FROM PAIN TO LOVE
Our Journey Outside the Rainbow

Naomi Wilma Scales & Marilyn Johnson Jordan

Copyright © 2021 Naomi Wilma Scales and Marilyn Johnson Jordan

Edited by Kocysha LaShaun of Be Accelerated into Purpose, LLC

Cover Design by Robert Matthews of intraVISION.net

All rights reserved. No part of this publication may be reproduced, distributed, or transmitted in any form or by any means, including photocopying, recording, or other electronic or mechanical methods, without the prior written permission of the publisher, except in the case of brief quotations embodied in critical reviews and certain other noncommercial uses permitted by copyright law. For permission requests, contact Naomi Wilma Scales and Marilyn Johnson Jordan at nwscalesandmjjordan@gmail.com.

DISCLAIMER

The story of our journey has been written to the best of our recollections and was not written to represent a verbatim transcript of conversations. We have retold these events the way we recall them. Some names and identifying details have been changed to protect the privacy of the people involved. Permission was granted for actual names used.

Material in this book may include information, products, or services by third parties. We, the authors, editor and publisher do not assume responsibility or liability for any third party material or opinions. Readers are advised to do their due diligence in making decisions.

We hope the reader finds in these pages the inspiration, laughter and words of wisdom that we intended to share, while enjoying the transparency.

Sincerely,
Naomi and Marilyn

ISBN: 9781736574904

DEDICATION

To Our Daughters
You have always been and will forever be our inspiration.
There would be no us without you. If we had to do it all
again, we would, with just as much, if not more vigor,
protection, and love.
We Love You!

****

Erin Lynn Ward - Goddaughter
Sept. 24, 1983 • July 30, 2020

Thank you for bravely living your life openly, with pride and
always being authentic. You have motivated us to embrace
who we are.

Gone Too Soon...
We Miss You!
Forever Rest in Love and Peace

CONTENTS

| | Acknowledgments | i |
| | Foreword | 1 |

SECTION ONE

1	Chapter 1 ~ HelMary	5
2	Chapter 2 ~ Pain	8
3	Chapter 3 ~ Different Worlds	16
4	Chapter 4 ~ That ONE Summer Day	26
5	Chapter 5 ~ That ONE Dreadful Night	30
6	Chapter 6 ~ Time to Get Out of Dodge	36
7	Chapter 7 ~ First Love	42

SECTION TWO

8	Chapter 8 ~ Where to Next	49
9	Chapter 9 ~ No "May" Flowers Here	53
10	Chapter 10 ~ A Little Bit of This, A Little Bit of That	75
11	Chapter 11 ~ Not Quite the Suga Daddy	98
12	Chapter 12 ~ A Life Taken, A Life Given	109
13	Chapter 13 ~ Secret Lovers	119
14	Chapter 14 ~ New Horizons	137

SECTION THREE

| 15 | Chapter 15 ~ The Choice | 146 |
| 16 | Chapter 16 ~ Yep! It's Happening | 155 |

17	Chapter 17 ~ Boot Camp	158
18	Chapter 18 ~ Times Have Changed	168
19	Chapter 19 ~ NOLA: Who Dat Land	179
20	Chapter 20 ~ California, USA	193
21	Chapter 21 ~ Boston, USA	203
22	Chapter 22 ~ The PACT	213

SECTION FOUR

23	Chapter 23 ~ Settling In	229
24	Chapter 24 ~ Diagnosed	235
25	Chapter 25 ~ A New Reality	242
26	Chapter 26 ~ Storm	252
27	Chapter 27 ~ Stage 5	267
28	Chapter 28 ~ Promises Made, Promises Kept	276
29	Chapter 29 ~ A Break in the Rainbow	288
30	Chapter 30 ~ Rainbow Complete	301
	Poem for My Mom	318

ACKNOWLEDGMENTS

To our incredible daughters and their devoted husbands, we love you so much and are very grateful for your genuine and unconditional love and encouraging support.

To our amazing family... siblings, aunts, uncles, cousins, nieces, nephews and our Goddaughters... Joy Massingill, Kema Ward-Hopper, and Erin Ward {Rest In Eternal Love} Thank you for all the ways you have shown us that we belong.

A huge thank you and kudos to our editor, Kocysha LaShaun, Founder of Be Accelerated into Purpose, LLC Author/Editor/Certified Spiritual Mindset Coach, for your dedicated patience, seeing our vision and working so hard to give it life.

Robert Matthews of Intravision created such a breath-taking cover design that mimicked exactly what we asked for and did it with ease and expediency.

Technodream Website Design endured our many frantic calls and never hesitated to appease with professionalism.

Thank you to our childhood friend, confidant, and Soror Carolyn Davis-Jones, CEO/Owner of Chance of a Lifetime Coaching. Your endorsement and support are eloquently and beautifully written in the foreword.

To our dedicated MarFran Cleaning employees, the hard work and commitment you give is invaluable.

To our pastors and therapists, we are grateful for your continued support and sound advice.

Naomi Wilma Scales and Marilyn Johnson Jordan

To our phenomenal readers, this is the first of many endeavors to come. We are thankful for you opening your hearts and minds to walk this journey with us.

The question... WHY NOW?

The answer... IT'S TIME!

To those that find a piece of you in this story;
Own it! Embrace it! Tell it! Live it Authentically!

FOREWORD

COVID-19 played ping-pong with our lives, causing a horrific pandemic killing thousands. If ever there was a time we needed to be *reconciled* or *introduced* to something totally revitalizing and refreshing, it is NOW! Leaving that up to Naomi Scales and Marilyn Jordan is breathtaking!

Bask in the excitement... embrace the spirit of vitality... grasp the healing power of the soul!

From Pain to Love: Our Journey Outside the Rainbow unequivocally loosens all the ties, grips and hang-ups of people who are facing the struggles (and in this case, hidden) of being totally **FREE** of who they are. It's more than a self-help and exhibits greater intensity than a passionate, emotional story.

This prolific piece of non-traditional art bridges the gap between who you were born to be, who you become, and most importantly, where you are most happy! It is here where Naomi and Marilyn intertwine experiences in four areas to becoming the best versions of themselves: (1) Early childhood (2) College life (3) Military life, and (4) Family life.

It's an awakening experience where you feel like yelling to the mountains every stressor that is scuffing out your shine. It's an awakening experience where you realize, 'WOW, I thought I was the only one that felt this way!' It's an awakening experience where you discover you really are more than enough!

There was always something compelling and mystical about Naomi, whom I affectionately call Wilma, ever since I met her as the girl from Chicago, over 30 years ago. She visited her grandmother each summer in Arkansas and brought so much dignity and pride to the south. We balanced well together and I am still beaming over the awesomeness of her asking me to eulogize her mother's homegoing. What an honor!

Since that very first day of kindergarten, I knew Marilyn would not only be my best friend, but also a trendsetter in her own rights. She only lasted a few weeks in that school simply because her *voice* made the difference. It was a lot bigger than her stature.

In 1983, Wilma, Marilyn and I embarked on our adult journey together at college. Frolicking through the streets of Conway, Arkansas, we turned corners others only dared to explore, and even created new adventures that taught us how to soar with our own wings! We became college friends, Sorority Sisters of Delta Sigma Theta Sorority, Inc., and now life-long collaborators!

Many are still searching for the resolution to resolve social indifferences in any manner. It is important to customize everything about your life. That is what takes place in *From Pain to Love: Our Journey Outside the Rainbow.*

As each page is turned, find yourself peeling off layer after layer of unwanted pain and grief. Seventeen years in the making, it is with genuine respect I choose to celebrate this non-traditional love story. It is also with great measure of merit and authenticity this foreword depicts for you to individually take bite-sized pieces of their dream to become palatable morsels for creating yours!

Carolyn Davis-Jones, MBA
CEO/Owner of Chance of a Lifetime Coaching
"Move Forward with Confidence"

SECTION ONE

Chapter 1 ~ HelMary

At 22 years old, she had three small children. The oldest child was seven years old – a boy – born when she was fifteen years old. I was next and two years later my sister arrived – all born before she turned twenty.

* * *

My mother was born in 1946 in the south. Her mom was a young lady raising three children while her husband was away fighting in a war for a country that did not even treat him as a person. My mom was the middle child of four siblings, a younger sister and brother and an older sister and brother.

My great-grandfather had Indian blood running through his veins and it reflected in my grandmother. He had long black hair, beautiful skin and high cheek bones – real American Indian features. Although my grandmother's children were beautiful, there was a concern for my mother because she did not speak until she was six or seven years old. Even then she still didn't speak much. She would sit long periods of time in silence. Unfortunately, those were things black families didn't speak on much at that time. There was no need to get her checked because whatever it was they felt she would be fine.

At 22 years old, she had three small children. The oldest child was seven years old – a boy – born when she was fifteen years old. I was next and two years later my sister arrived – all born before she turned twenty. We lived with my grandmother in a shotgun house, who also had two of her five children living there. Rumors had it that my grandmother, at times, had an enigmatic personality. I never saw this side as a grandchild because she treated us good.

My mom decided she would go to Chicago with her childhood friend, Karen, find a good job, get settled in, and then send for us. When she sent for us, we moved in with Karen and her little sister. Karen had no children, but she treated us like her own. We would always go to Arkansas in the summer to be with our grandmother until their schools started and then head back to Chicago.

It was the summer of '71 when we returned to Chicago that things would change. How little did we know just how much that change would affect our lives for many years to come. The *change* that was about to happen may have been the major contributing factor to the dysfunction of our unit.

~MJ's Journey~

I was a pre-menopausal baby. At the ripe age of 43, my mother had already given birth to my five siblings and then came surprise baby number six – ME! My upbringing was different from theirs on so many levels because my dad was 13 years my mom's senior. They were also much older than my friend's parents. My mother, Mary, raised by a very strict grandmother, was always resentful to her mother for choosing a lifestyle that did not quite include the rearing of a little girl. In spite of the strained relationship between them, I had a very special bond with my grandmother and enjoyed every moment spent with her. Since all my siblings were much older than me, it often felt like I was an only child. I was very close to the middle siblings – a sister who was seven years older and a brother who was 16 years old when I was born. My relationship with those two was unique because they were present during most of my molding years. Regardless of all our ages, one thing was understood about our foundation. Religion, church and our faith were to always supersede any decision and lifestyle choices made. Church was our life and we literally spent more time in the church building than we did anywhere else.

Chapter 2 ~ Pain

After I would rub up against [his] penis, making it hard, he would then masturbate in front of me. I guess everything gets old after a while... having an eight-year-old child observe you pleasuring yourself was not stimulating anymore. He now wanted me to...

* * *

My mama had gotten married to a man with a good job and benefits! She had found love over the summer of '71 and this man wanted to take care of her and her three children. We got the good news while we were still in Arkansas. We knew when we returned to Chicago we would no longer be living with Karen. We now had a new house and a new stepdaddy.

It was a beautiful two-story house with a basement in a nice, middle-class neighborhood on the south side of Chicago on 74th and May – not too far from Alonzo Stagg High School Football Stadium. Purchasing a home was a great accomplishment for my mom. The house was big enough for each of us to have our own room. The extra bonus of the move was that my uncle lived across the street. He wasn't my blood uncle, but his brother was my grandmother's live-in-boyfriend, who we considered our grandaddy. Even though the neighborhood was nice, it was still Chicago. Since we were the new kids on the block, every day we were challenged on the way we talked and looked. We had to defend ourselves in the street, but little did we know how that battle would be small compared to the battle to fight within our own home.

In the beginning, I didn't know what type of relationship my mom and her husband, Hank, had. I knew my mom could be volatile at times, plenty damn mean, and she took no shit from anyone. It was also during this time when my brother started getting in trouble. As I think back and recollect my thoughts to put these words on paper, I don't know if my memories of my brother were worse *before* or *after* this man came into our lives.

One day Hank brought home a puppy to teach my brother some responsibilities. My brother would have to take the puppy out for walks. One day our stepdad decided to go walking with them. This became an every night thing. I assumed this was their time to connect and develop a relationship. I really didn't care because it meant our brother wasn't bothering us and this would become my bonding time with my sister. We were each other's best friend, playing all the time and not really paying attention to the relationship between our stepdad and brother.

As time went on, I started to notice a look on my brother's face. A look I could not really understand at the time, but it was a look of fear sometimes mixed with pain and a hollow stare. He had started becoming much angrier, which was a little troubling. Recognizing his aggressiveness and with a stepdad in the picture, I think my mom could sense how this could get ugly.

As we neared the end of another school year, after which we'd make our usual summer trip to Arkansas, it was becoming a lot tougher to ignore my brother's behavior. Becoming more defiant, he would be gone for days at a time. As troubling as all that was, this now meant our stepdad would turn his attention to me and my sister. For some reason a man who had a good job always seemed to be home, especially right after school – and before my mom got home. We would come in from school and he would want to hear about our day.

Eventually, he only wanted to hear about *my* day. Then he only wanted to hear about *my* day in *his* room. He would ask me to touch him, but with his pants on. He'd say, "Just rub up against the balls and make 'em hard." I was only eight years old at the time and I can't remember exactly what he said to make me not tell my mom. It never crossed my mind to tell her because I thought she would do something from being angry and make us lose the house and I knew she loved this house.

If I had told her, I'm sure we would all have to go back to

Karen's, or worse – back to Arkansas. I never thought my mom would be mad at me. However, I always thought that I was protecting her. As far back as I can remember, I was crazy about my mom; I simply adored her. She was a special kind of pretty to me and I was very protective of her. It was almost as if I had a crush on her. She was really my first love.

After I would rub up against Hank's penis, making it hard, he would then masturbate in front of me. I guess that got old and not stimulating enough after a while – just having an eight-year-old child *observe* him pleasuring himself. He now wanted me to suck his penis and he would put my mouth on it. Since I was clearly not telling my mom what he was doing, he felt emboldened to try and penetrate me with his penis. He would promise it would not hurt because he would only put the tip of it in my vagina. I would cry in the beginning, but soon I stopped crying because then he wanted my little sister to watch. I knew that would inevitably lead to him trying to hurt her.

I was awakened one night from my sleep by a knocking noise. I got up and ran into the hallway toward the noise to find my mother and her little sister dragging Hank down the stairs beating the shit out of him. Hank hit my mother. Her baby sister asked, "What the heck is wrong with you?" Hank attempted to swing on my aunt. It was at that point the fear

I'd carried inside would manifest. *That side* would come out of Helen on that night. I always feared her dark side. She would take mess from guys, sometimes she would give it back and at times she'd give it to them for no reason. But what Helen did not do was allow anyone to mistreat someone she loved, and she loved her little sister. My Aunt Heavenly and her best friend Patsy had come to Chicago to visit and hang out with my mom, maybe even move there.

Hank and Helen would fight and argue all the time. The fights could get bad sometimes with screaming and cussing. My mother had a deep rooted anger in her and she could say some of the worst things. She was what many would call a "bad chick". I do not know why they were fighting on this night, but it was bad. I had a theory about why they were fighting, but at the time I didn't know for sure. I would eventually find out the real reason years later.

See, my Aunt Heavenly was gorgeous and a little shy. You know, "the quiet one", who most people believe won't tell when shit happens to them. I think my stepdad had made a move on my aunt. My aunt was young, only thirteen years older than me. This night the argument spilled out into the hallway. There had been many nights of arguing, then loud noises of thumps and pushing. My sister and I had accepted this as a normal part of being a family, but this night everyone had enough.

My mom screamed, "Go across the street and get your Uncle Oscar and take your sister." I grabbed my sister by the arm and we ran across the street to Uncle Oscar's house crying and screaming, "They need help." He asked, "Who?" "Helen and Heavenly (we called our mother by her first name as "mama" was reserved for our grandmother). He is fighting them."

My uncle turned to his wife, Kat, and said, "Put the girls in the bed." He went to his room and got his pistol. He went across the street mad as hell. By the time he got there, they were at the bottom of the stairs. Uncle Oscar said, "You raise your hand again and I will put your ass to sleep forever. Now get your ass up and get the hell out of here before I get mad." My Aunt Kat called the police and by the time they arrived, my uncle hid his gun. When old stepdaddy told the police that Uncle Oscar had a gun, my mom, aunts and uncle said he was a damn liar and an abuser.

So old man Hank was hauled off to jail for the night. Helen was done now; she'd had enough. During this time, my mom stopped paying the house note and we ended up living with Uncle Oscar and Aunt Kat. Karen was not going to let her girl be out there like that, so we moved back in with her. Karen had a new man in her life. He was an exceptionally good man who wanted Karen to be happy, and having Helen and her kids around made Karen happy.

Although we had to share a room at Karen's, it was cool because it meant no more of Hank terrorizing my mom and torturing my brother. Of course, the best part of moving back with Karen was that my sister and I would no longer be subjected to Hank's perverted mind and unthinkable acts of child molestation.

~MJ's Journey~

Meanwhile, back in Arkansas... Daddy passed when I was ten years old. It was challenging for me when mama started dating. We would go to her boyfriend's ranch for weekend visits. I loved riding the horses, but I did not enjoy the rides that her boyfriend had in mind. He was no longer the nice, old man with horses, gifts and plenty of money. Instead, he became the nasty, old man that promised me these things for a price. The weekend getaways became stressful. The visits were later coupled with me fighting in my sleep and always with one eye open. His game of ride-the-pony no longer involved the animal in the barn, but instead just the one in the house – HIM!

I did not tell my mom because I wanted to see her happy. Making her smile was always my ultimate goal. Her being proud of me is also why I tried to remain committed to the piano lessons. I was trying to make it work, but after more than a couple of teachers, the piano keys were not the only thing being stroked. Here I was, again, at the hands of a man where there should have been peace. Even though I never chose to tell my mom any of the horrific things done to me at the hands of these trusted adults, I managed to outwardly display a decent amount of joy. This joy was layered with resentment and at times a nasty attitude.

I thought what was happening to me was my fault. I could make no sense of why two respectable and upstanding men in the community would want to fondle and force themselves on me if it wasn't something that was supposed to be.

Mama's boyfriend breakup and the cancellation of the piano lessons somehow made me a virgin again. Finally, I was an innocent little girl that had lost a small portion of her childhood. It quickly became evident that there are things we expect to find peace in doing, can instead bring chaos and confusion.

Chapter 3 ~ Different Worlds

When I made it home, I was looking a hot mess. My hair was all over my head – what little hair I had left and what was not pulled out...

* * *

Even though we stayed with my uncle and Karen after losing the house, my mom had signed up for public housing because she wasn't making enough to afford a decent place. However, there was a waiting list, so we also moved from apartment to apartment while waiting to be placed. When our number was finally called, we moved into the Chicago Public Housing known as "the projects" at 2330 South State Street where the Harold Ickes Projects was located.

As it relates to the Ickes, there was a quiet craziness about it, yet it was probably one of the mildest projects to move into. It was not on the west side and it was not the Stateway Gardens (now Park Boulevard), but it was the projects nonetheless – a place which revealed a whole new level of cruelty and meanness. Thankfully, it was also not the Cabrini-Green's. We would be horrified everyday about news of the vilest stuff in the world happening to the people there. This environment in the projects was different than any I had ever heard or seen before – literally, with families living on top of each other. It was the survival of the toughest in the Ickes.

Some days I was up for the fight and other days it was just a matter of making it out alive from building to building. This is one reason I always looked forward to the summers in Arkansas to be with my grandmother, aunts and cousins. We usually would go by bus or my great-aunt would drive us. However we got there, we were glad to be there and away from the projects.

Gun shots in the projects were not unusual, but one time was different. Word started to get around that someone had gotten shot the night before and we all thought it was gang-related. This time it was not a gang banger, but it was gang-related. It was a good kid just standing in front of his building shot by a bullet meant for one of his gang-banging cousins. A decent kid shot, standing in the right place at the wrong time. Charles was my age, in school and doing things that usually kept you out of trouble and gangs respected that. For a while, we were all scared because we figured if Charles could get shot, anyone could, especially during that period.

It was during a time when the Vice Lords, the Blackstone Rangers (Stones) and Disciples were the three major gangs in Chicago. There were more, but these were the ones that were active in our community. The Vice Lords were about business. As a matter of fact, they opened businesses like restaurants, clothing boutiques, pool rooms and an art studio. In addition, they offered many programs for the benefit of the community. The Vice Lords didn't recruit, but guys would flock to them in a strange and peculiar way. The Vice Lords were almost like a privileged few. They were the forerunners to change the image of street gangs. Two southside street gangs started to form what would eventually evolve into two of the most powerful street organizations in Chicago. They were the Blackstone Rangers and the Black Disciples. But even with that said, there was a structure and a way of doing things. Charles' shooting was a mistake. The wrong person was shot and it put fear into all of us.

Most of our problems, however, came from playground fights, bullying and after school altercations. I was a bit of a tomboy and a little on the rough side and had my share of weekly fights after school, mainly with boys because girls wouldn't take a chance. For some reason guys always challenged me. I thought maybe it was because my hair was short and I looked like a boy.

~MJ's Journey~

My upbringing was quite the opposite. Living on a hill in an eight room home with a white picket fence, surrounded by honeysuckle bushes, banana plants, walnut and pecan trees was the dream of so many. At times, I did not know how to appreciate what I had. I spent the majority of my days and had the best times at the shotgun houses with no grass. I never understood why hanging out with "those" friends was not encouraged. What was different – especially since they spent as much time in church praying, shouting and Bible toting as we did. Isn't that what makes you right? Or was it because they weren't sending their children to college? Maybe it could have been that their family didn't own or manage a black business or coordinate damn near every racial-related boycott and protest in the community. Never understood it then. Still don't now. Primarily, because most of that was why so many didn't like me. It did help that my childhood was full of busyness.

I was actively involved in numerous church activities and community organizations. My fondest memories were the trips with the prayer club band. I looked forward to my weekly pickup for the Wednesday prayer meetings with my church girlfriends. We would also travel each month with one of the missionary women to the nursing homes and sing to the residents that were celebrating birthdays. This was the highlight of my first Saturday of the month. Afterwards, she would take us to the Burger Ranch or to the Buccaneer for a good ole soft serve ice cream cone. She often hosted sleepovers for us and taught about inappropriate behavior, what was acceptable and what wasn't, as it related to boys. The lessons often included what was considered ladylike behavior and how to display good manners.

I also enjoyed staying busy in the Federated Club and its many oratorical competitions. I placed several times in the speaking category, winning many certificates and trophies. My proudest win was second place in the singing category. I divided my time with these activities, along with Girl Scouts. Scouting was challenging because I was being bullied by one of the girls. Because *of that, I would dread the meetings. I tried to enjoy Girl Scout cookie time and I was one of the top sellers. That brought on double anxiety because I always wanted to be number one in everything I did. However, the bully wasn't having it without tormenting me.*

The fights with boys were usually a result of them teasing because that's just what boys do. For some reason though, one day I had gotten the attention of the baddest girl in school. I knew she was a bad ass. Maybe because it was picture day and I was all dressed up. I don't know why this day but she had made it clear that she was going to kick my butt after school.

I was never nervous or scared to fight a boy because boys were predictable. All I had to do was wait for them to swing and I would do like I had seen in boxing and wrestling on TV and just bob and weave. Sometimes I would duck under their swing, come right under their legs and power drive them down and with all my force, start pounding their face into the ground. Fighting boys was just like fighting my brother, which I did all the time. I would fight him with all my power and strength to the point he would try and inflict real pain on me. For instance, he threw an afro pick at me, so the spokes from the pick stuck into my foot. I, on the other hand, would pick up things like hot grease, whatever was near me, because my rage for him was so embedded in my soul that my spirit would literally leave my body whenever we'd fight.

Some acts are never forgotten and never forgiven until one of the parties departs the earth.

Fighting a girl would be a challenge, especially since it was picture day and I had on a dress. A dress is something I hated to wear and would cry and get terribly upset whenever I had to wear one. I had on this stupid dress with a scarf attached to it and my hair had been straightened. The word had started to circulate that I was the next one in the barrel for a beating by the baddest girl in school. I had a saving grace this day because another bad ass girl in my class named Ramona wanted to fight for me because she wanted to beat Felicia down. She would have because among all the girls at our school, Ramona was the real one that no one messed with. In her eyes, I was cool, so I was good to go. She had my back that day and she was going to take care of my little problem.

It was 2:15 pm and school was about to let out at 3:00 pm. I relaxed and started talking mess because I knew I didn't have to fight Felicia. It wasn't that I was scared or maybe deep down inside I was a little intimidated, but I didn't think or care at that time because I was covered. Two-thirty hits and Ramona is called to the office and given detention because of a fight she'd been in earlier that week. Felicia started licking her chops. She knew she had a scary chick on her hand. She didn't know if I could fight girls like I fought boys, but she wanted to find out. Honestly, I cannot remember if I had ever fought a girl before.

She sensed I did not want any part of her. When the bell rang it was time to go home and the crowd was lining up to see the fight because that is how it went. A circle would form around the two participants. As soon as I hit the yard, she grabbed me by my scarf and I reacted. I grabbed her and that is all I remember. I got a total ass whooping that day on the school yard. My best friend told me she was trying to make it through the crowd, but she saw where I had her by the collar and all I needed to do was pull her down and start stomping her.

I was the laughingstock of the school yard. The word got around quickly. My little sister got the word and was devastated. She expressed to me that the fight had to be uneven because there was no way I had lost to a girl. Someone had to have jumped in, I was double teamed, or something, but none of that happened. I received a total beat down fair and square. My pride was hurt and my shield as a warrior was now compromised. From that day on, I had to prove myself all over again at school and on the playground.

When I made it home, I was looking a hot mess. My hair was all over my head – what little hair I had left that was not pulled out in the fight. My dress was ripped and that scarf – I had no idea where the hell it was. My sister had a look on her face like, "What just happened?" Because we could not rely on our brother, I was the protector. I think she was more upset with me losing my status as a bad ass, rather than the pain I was going through at the time.

My mother came home and I was sitting in my room, drowning in my tears and loathing in self-pity. She looked at me with worry on her face and asked what was wrong. Sniffling with tears running down my face, I told her I had been in a fight and had lost. I used the words, "I got beat up." She yelled with rage and worry in her voice, "Who jumped you and how many?" I said one. My mom said, "Okay, boy or girl?" As the tip of my tongue started with the letter "G", she interrupted me and screamed, "A GIRL?" I said yes. I could see a shift in her body language as she asked with attitude, "How old was she?" I proceeded with caution because this was obviously no longer about my pain or the fact that I thought I had been done wrong. I said in the most pitiful and beaten down voice as possible, "My age."

Her yell was so loud it seemed as though it was coming from a bull horn. "*Your* age?" A slew of questions then spurred from her mouth, "Did she have a knife? Did someone jump in?" And on and on until finally, after I had repeatedly said no, she yelled, "Then shut the fuck up and wipe those tears from your eyes and get yourself together! Because now you have to prove every day to those bitches in these 'jets' that you are not a punk ass." I realized at that time I had to fight and fight with all I had. I needed to prove to all that I was not that chick they thought I was.

The fights continued and I won 95% of them, but more than anything, I had regained my confidence and my respect back on the school yard. I had earned my throne as the "Queen of Bring It On". My little sister did not have that look in her face anymore, that look of insecurity and fear. She thought I was an invincible bad ass and that was essential to us surviving in the Ickes. There was no such thing as a *hunting season*. Every day, every minute, every second was hunting season. You either got destroyed or became prey for someone to beat on you every day. I was not going to allow myself or my little sister to become prey. Oh, and I did find out two years later that Felicia was arrested for murder. She was only thirteen or fourteen.

~MJ's Journey~

My family received a certain level of respect from adults due to our economic status, but what brought them respect brought me resentment. I was a victim of bullying because of what my family had, what I looked like and what I wore. I will never forget one of the most pivotal encounters with a set of bullies known as the Harmony sisters. When they jumped me, it was obviously well planned and executed. They were both standing in the opening of the bathroom stall when I stepped out. They told me I needed to either cut my hair or give them my leather patchwork jacket, otherwise they would jump me. I thought I was being given options when actually two of the three things happened anyway. They pulled my hair and pushed me out the restroom door. I fell into the hall as they took my jacket. I just remember bragging how they didn't get the matching purse. I mean, what else is there to say when you're lying in the hall with strings of your hair on the floor while hanging on to your favorite patchwork leather clutch?

Chapter 4 ~ That ONE Summer Day

It was seven years later when we formally met, and I realized the feeling I felt that one summer day at the age of 13, would be one that I would never ever be able to shake.

* * *

One summer, while in Arkansas, I was running to the corner store to get some things for my grandmother and I stopped in my tracks when I saw her. I had made it to the store and there was a nice car sitting in front. I knew the car because it was one that had been to my grandmother's house before, but *she* was sitting on the passenger side. I looked over into the car, saw her smiling and my heart literally skipped a beat. I was like, 'Oh boy, what kind of feeling is this?'

I had seen many girls and even admired their appearance, but her looks captivated my mind for days. Hell, my best friend in Arkansas was a beautiful girl. I had beautiful girls in my family, but this girl's beauty had reached down into my chest and grabbed me by the lungs and took my breath away. Her skin looked so soft – a chocolate brown milkshake kind of look. Even though I'd heard about her before now, this was the first time I had seen her face.

She was from a genuinely nice and well-to-do black family in town. But my best friend at the time had a crush on her boyfriend, which made her enemy number one. One day it was supposed to be our mission to beat her up, or at least separate her from her man by telling her to "quit him now". We had gone to his house and knocked on the door because we were told she would be there, but she was not there and that was the end of that. Yet, here I was staring, and I didn't even speak to her – only her boyfriend. I knew him because he was my uncle's best friend and practically family.

She gave a party a few weeks later for her 13th birthday, but we were not invited. She lived only a few blocks from my grandmother's house, so my best friend and our crew decided we would crash the party. We headed down there to just jump in and start partying with everyone. Her mom knew we were not supposed to be there, but when she saw us, she stayed cool and didn't make a big deal about it. She was a kind and very sweet girl, but I didn't say anything to her that day either.

~MJ's Journey~

There she was! The girl I had seen in front of the neighborhood corner grocery store while in the car with my boyfriend, was now crashing my birthday party. She had come with a group of people that had not been invited and neither had she. I was a little excited. I mean, who doesn't want EVERYBODY to celebrate them? While excited, I was also nervous. At the time, I thought the nerves were because these were children that my mama did not know. That was always a big no-no. If she didn't know them, they were not welcome. I was praying that mama would approve, since it was an outdoor party. My birthday party was always a big deal even though a summer birthday never guaranteed that the word would get out. Mama always wanted to send invitations instead of word of mouth, or pass out flyers like most kids did. My 13th birthday party had more people than any I'd ever had. I remember making eye contact with her, but the vibe was different than the one I received when we first saw each other. I dismissed it all and decided that I misread something and figured she just wanted to be my friend.

It was seven years later when we formally met, and I realized the feeling I felt that one summer day at the age of 13 would be one that I would never ever be able to shake. I thought she was beautiful. I realized what it meant when someone said a person's beauty could be breathtaking. It was the kind of beauty that could only be accompanied with a kind soul.

One of the things I enjoyed most about going to Arkansas were the people. We would play all day and night outside with our friends. This would be the time we would also attend church. We learned that we were children of God and that if we SINNED; hell was waiting on us. Vacation Bible School is where I first learned about some of my mother's demons. All I knew is that I loved my mother very much and I was always afraid of her not loving me. To me, my mother was the one who loved me more than anyone in my family. I know that sounds strange because your mom is supposed to love you, but because we were basically reared by our grandmother and aunts; they were essentially our mother as well.

One summer at Vacation Bible School in Little Rock, Arkansas, my cousin told me a story that involved my mom and my sister's father. Although my mother did not graduate from high school, she went to barber's school in Little Rock. It was during this time she met my sister's father, a young stunning man with a future in local politics. Helen was an extremely attractive young lady and very shapely. After having many sexual encounters with her, he decided to end the relationship and became very ugly acting in his treatment of her. This didn't sit well with Helen and she reacted violently and threatened him and his family. She was forced to leave Little Rock due to a restraining order and was basically escorted out of town. My mother was always seeking the attention of older men and she had this deep rooted anger that would come in rages of fits that was aimed at whoever was in her path. She cussed, threw things, would always seek revenge when she felt threatened and harmed. My brother's father and my father were much older than Helen. The men that impregnated her were not only much older than her, they also had violent tendencies, especially my brother's father.

Chapter 5 ~ That ONE Dreadful Night

The body needed to be identified at the morgue and my mom was listed as next of kin. Ken had come to take her and to be by her side. After they identified the body, he took her home and stayed to comfort her.

* * *

My mom worked odd jobs and received financial help from her family. Sometimes her work would bring her home late at night and I kept thinking to myself, if we could leave the Ickes, I would no longer have to wait up for her to come home. I was always fearful of her coming to the building by herself or simply just walking from a cab or the bus. There would be several occasions when the elevator was not working and we lived on the ninth floor. Those nights gave me the most feelings of helplessness.

When she would call on her break, I would always ask her what time she was getting off. I wanted to make sure the time hadn't changed from her original schedule. This would allow me to calculate her bus ride time, so I could determine when she should get home. I would literally start walking halfway down the stairs just in case I could meet her as she climbed up. I only remember maybe two times meeting her on the stairs. She laughed the first time and told me to stay in the apartment because she was grown and could take care of herself. Since she was laughing, I did not take her seriously, but she meant that. She let me know just how serious she was the next time. After that, I never met her on the stairs again.

During the times the elevator wasn't working, I would pray because my family in Arkansas told me if I prayed to God, He would take care of my worries and concerns. I prayed like I had been taught. This particular night it was getting later than usual. I wasn't too worried about it or thinking much of it because DePaul University basketball was on. They were playing a big game and had won. I was so excited. As I reached to turn the television off, a news report came across the screen of a murder in Skokie, Illinois. Skokie is about 25 minutes outside of Chicago. It was in Skokie and not Chicago. It was a woman at her home in her gown, so I knew it was not my mom.

I turned off the TV and went to bed. The next morning, I wanted to tell my mom about the game. I knocked on her bedroom door and she asked me to wait. I could tell she had company. It did not bother me that my mom had male company, especially if they were making sure that she made it up the stairs when the elevator wasn't working. She told me to go to the store and buy a newspaper. I took the money off the kitchen table, headed to the corner store and grabbed a paper. When I returned, her friend was gone. I sat out by her door, as I did quite often, waiting for a chance to chat with her about what was going on. She asked me to come in her room and I gave her the paper, except the sports section because that is what we did. I took my usual spot at the foot of her bed.

She said with a painful tone in her voice – one I had never heard before – "Karen was killed last night." I had never seen my mother cry, not even after some of her fights with her male friends. She was the toughest and strongest person I knew. Yet there she was with tears in her eyes and voice trembling, as I said loudly and a bit confused, "WHO?" She repeated her name again. "Karen." All that could come out of my mouth was "Who?" Of course, I knew who Karen was. She was my mother's best friend, her moral compass, her dearest and realest friend.

They had come to Chicago together as two girls on a mission to make it in the big city. Karen was the friend, who no matter what was going on in her life, if my mother needed her, she would drop it all and come running (especially for Helen's children). We were never told Karen was our Godmother, but it was clear if anything ever happened to my mom, everyone was to make sure the authorities found Karen.

My mom started crying and she couldn't get her words together. Karen understood my mom and could calm her down when no other person could. She loved her unconditionally and now she was gone. While hoping for a better life, but that place had to include a man. They dated all type of men, but felt a certain kind of affinity toward older men. Karen spent years with an older man. He had taken good care of her and made sure that her friend, Helen, was taken care of as well. He paid Karen's rent while he maintained his house with his wife and children. Karen made sure that we knew we always had a place to live.

After years of being with a married man, who would never leave his wife, Karen had finally found love with a man who, she thought, wanted to marry her. He told her he was single. He had a high-paying job and plenty of prestige. All he needed was a woman by his side. We had only met him once, and to us he was Uncle Victor. Whenever Karen would come to see us, after she started dating Victor, she would always bring nice things and had the best and finest cars. She was always a kind and gentle soul, but this new her with money was something to witness.

She shared her new riches with my mom and her sister. Karen was the glue that was holding it all together for the girls from Arkansas, but her new beau had a side to him a lot of us didn't know about. Karen was murdered while answering the door of her nice Chicago suburban home. She answered the door in her night gown, thinking it was someone she knew. She was shot several times at close range. It was later determined that Victor owed money to people, a lot of money. They did not want him dead, but instead they wanted to send him a message. His name was not even the name we were told to call him. He was living under an alias because he had a wife and a family. He was running from a previous life and whatever that previous life was, it found him that night.

The evening of Karen's murder, my mom was finishing her shift. When she walked through the door to leave, standing in the hallway was Ken. Ken was the married man Karen had spent years with. He had taken good care of her and her family. My mom knew it was bad news immediately. She knew it was not one of us because it would've been Karen standing in that hallway, and not Ken.

The body needed to be identified at the morgue and my mom was listed as next of kin. Ken had come to take her and to be by her side. After they identified the body, he brought her home and stayed by her side all night. I do not think I ever really realized the depth of my mom and Karen's friendship. Karen was her ride or die chick. They had made this move together to Chicago and now Karen was gone, and in such a violent way.

Chicago was a tough city. They had their battles, but had

established themselves as country girls that could hold their own in the big city. Only to lose Karen when she finally found what they both wanted so desperately – a man. Had their quest for a man been the death of her? Was their search for a man blinded by a need to be wanted? My mom's marriage to Hank was riddled with abuse and Karen's marriage ended her life.

Soon after, we finally left the Ickes. We moved to 43rd and King Drive, still on the south side, into a nice three-story apartment. Our stay in the Ickes was supposed to be temporary, but we stayed there for years.

I do not think my mom ever found that kind of love from a friend like Karen again. She was there for us every time we faced being in the street. Her death touched my mom in a way I don't think she ever recovered from.

Chapter 6 ~ Time to Get Out of Dodge

When my mother got to the hospital, she looked scared, but she wasn't crying. She was looking at me and smiling telling me, "I'm so glad you are okay. You are going to be okay. You are fine; we are going home."

* * *

After being stabbed during a fight downtown, I had made up my mind that I was leaving Chicago. I had received several stitches after fighting off a thug and his thuggish girls. They jumped me and two of my friends from high school, when we were downtown hanging out on the first day of spring break. As much as we tried to avoid fighting them, we became prey for the day. It had been years since leaving the Ickes, but the instinct to fight when enticed was not gone.

They followed us from State Street to Michigan Avenue. Out of nowhere, the guy in the group bumped into me. I remained quiet the first time. Then he did it again. By this time, it was be punked or fight. Thank God one of my friends felt the same way. If not, I would not be here today to complete this journey. The second time I said, "Watch where you are going bitch!" Everyone in the hood knows when you call a boy a bitch, those are fighting words.

He swung and hit me in the face. I was stung and dazed, but not out. My two friends started fighting his girls. One of my friends, Vanessa, was doing such a great job serving a beatdown, that one of the thug chicks decided she needed to pull out a knife and cut Vanessa on her chin. I was left fighting the guy and I do mean I was fighting. I was kicking his butt up one side of the street and down the other. Our other friend decided it was time for her to run after Vanessa was cut.

Vanessa and I battled and fought our way around to the side of a building of a construction site. I could hear my mother's voice in my ear, "Do whatever you need to do to survive." I knew if I could get him near a fence at the construction site I could leverage my strength against his. I couldn't continue to fight him because I was getting tired, but I knew I had to weaken his strength. I did my under punch move, which I had mastered from my days in the Ickes fighting boys all day long. I got under his body and got my legs under him. My legs were my strength because of my butt. I drove him into the fence. I had him pinned against it and my body was into him and he couldn't swing, so I was beating him in his face. I was choking, punching, and biting him while doing whatever I had to do to survive. Then out of nowhere one of his girls appeared.

I thought they were busy fighting my girls but apparently one was free now to jump in and double team me. At first, she was standing back yelling at him, "Get her!" Cars drove by and no one stopped to intervene. As a matter of fact, people started yelling, "Beat his ass." I think people thought it was two boys fighting cause surely people would not be encouraging a fight between a girl and a boy.

I just wanted to survive. The girl yelling decided it was time to jump in. I was able to kick her off me. He was still pinned up against the fence. I figured if I knocked his ass out, his girl would go away. I guess he had enough of getting his ass kicked, so he then screamed to his girl, "Stab this bitch!" WHAT THE HELL!

I didn't know they had a knife. I'm thinking to myself, 'Did he just say, "Stab this bitch?"' I had to get the hell out of there. She jumped on my back, while I punched him in his nut sack with all my force. He fell to the ground. I then hit her so hard she dropped the knife and hit the ground like a piece of paper falling to the floor. I was able to break free and run away.

As I was running from them, Vanessa and I ran into each other. She knew she had to find me because we never left each other behind. We then ran into the first hotel lobby that was open for us to get in and the other friend was already there. I was relieved that we'd all made it safely. I was extremely tired and sweat was running down my back. Vanessa asked if I was okay. I said, "I'm fine, just tired.

"Then I told her my back was full of sweat. She looked at it and screamed, "You're bleeding!"

The hotel called the police, but told us we had to get out of the lobby. We waited for the police outside not knowing if the thug and his girls had left the scene or not. Luckily, they had left. Once we made it to the hospital, I found out I'd been stabbed in the back near my right shoulder. I received 22 stitches. The doctor told me I was a lucky girl because if I had turned around the blade would've gone straight through my heart. He said, "Young lady, you have an angel watching over you." Vanessa had been cut on her face and needed stitches as well. The other friend was fine because she had taken off immediately from the get-go.

I was in tremendous pain and my arm felt like someone was twisting their fist inside of it. When my mother got to the hospital, she looked scared but wasn't crying. She smiled as she looked at me, saying how glad she was that I was okay. I saw that the tears she cried on her way to me had gathered in the corner of her eyes. I felt safe again because she was there and I could feel that she was proud of me and thankful that I had survived.

I didn't want to go home until I knew Vanessa was okay. I asked repeatedly if she was fine and they told me she had been asking the same about me. Vanessa and I were a part of an incredibly special group of friends. We had bonded in high school because we were all in a special principal scholar program. We had decided we'd have each other's back always, no matter what. It didn't necessarily mean fighting; it just meant we would take care of each other. That incident scared me and made me petrified to leave my apartment the entire spring break. I kept thinking every time I'd go outside that I'd get jumped on or stabbed.

So yeah, after this, I was ready to get the heck out of Chicago. I'd had more than enough of my share of heartaches and trauma, including the snatching of pure innocence as a child at the hands of Hank. There were other memories of incidents constantly occupying my brain – incidents that made me question my own importance, my confidence, and whether or not anyone cared about me. Then there was my brother.

My brother was never available to protect me and my sister from the constant fights we endured. Nor did he bother to stop the sexual abuse from a neighborhood boy when asked. As he was dealing with his own demons, we had to fight him as much as we fought in the street because he often took his anger out on us.

I felt a little guilty about wanting to get out of Chicago because I'd be leaving my family behind. Things were changing as my brother had met a girl who was pregnant and having my first nephew. Even though he'd caused a lot of pain in our family, he was still our mother's son. She made it crystal clear that we were to stick together from the moment we moved to Chicago.

Chapter 7 ~ First Love

My high school boyfriend and I were an item all of my early dating years. Although we spent more time making up than we did dating, I felt that he had to be the one.

* * *

Although ready to leave Chicago, there was one person who brought light to my life. We met before my senior year of high school when I was working a summer job. I don't know if we were boyfriend and girlfriend because we'd just met, but his name was Chris. He was tall and handsome, with caramel brown skin. He spoke with such calmness and always complimented me on my shape and how smart I was. He always listened to my crazy ideas about what I wanted to do with my life. He was an only child – just him and his mom. He was planning to attend Eastern Illinois University when he graduated from high school.

I'd had a lot of boyfriends growing up, some in Arkansas and some in Chicago, but Chris was different. He was so gentle and he treated my body with such respect. Because I didn't want to, we didn't have sex immediately. Every time I'd slept with someone, it would end any kind of feelings I had for them because I never felt like I was there; it was always just a job or a mission.

Not so with Chris. I enjoyed talking to and spending time with him. He was smart, taught me about the nontraditional sports he played and shared several of his books with me. I learned so much from him and did not want to lose our friendship. He was my secret. I did not want to tell any of my friends about him because I thought he would like them more and lose interest in me. It was then when I realized just how my childhood imagination had prepared me for this.

I worked hard at learning about the world – not just learning what was in the textbooks, but things that could take me to a magical place. I had finally found a friend who also had a vivid imagination and believed in the unreachable and he was a guy. We both knew our education would be the key to leading us to those fantasy filled places, but we had to be able to hold conversations of worldly knowledge.

One afternoon he kissed me on the lips; it felt different. I knew this would mess up everything, but I let him kiss me anyway. He placed his hand on my small breasts and touched me with gentleness. I waited for him to pull out his penis and do the regular, but he was not regular. He kissed me from my neck to my breasts and I thought, 'Okay this is different.' Then he kept going lower and lower. His wet tongue was kissing my clit and I felt something I had never felt before. He was pleasing me with compassion and care. This was definitely a game changer.

That entire afternoon was special because my body felt good and not like all the other times. I left feeling like I would marry Chris, or at least find a husband like him. Our relationship went on for the entire summer before our senior year. Our encounters were beautiful and special to me. I did have a boyfriend at the time, but to me Chris was my man. I loved him because he was incredible. I felt in my heart he would make someone a terrific husband because he made this insecure and fragile little girl feel like she was being seen for the first time in her life.

In a strange way, I felt Chris recognized my pain and never wanted to mislead me. He could feel the suffering in my heart, but I also believed he came into my life to help me recover from the pain my body had felt. He opened my heart to know how I should be treated. As I write this on paper, I don't know that I ever realized it was Chris who helped me identify my true sexuality. Even if I could love Chris, I could never be in love with him. He knew this and I knew this, but he was still my very first love. During this time, I decided that was how I would pursue love. Sex would come and go, but only LOVE would take up space in my soul.

~MJ's Journey~

My high school boyfriend and I were an item all of my early dating years. Although we spent more time making up than actually dating, it seemed as though not being an item was not an option. Our spats were sometimes small, but definitely often. Since we had been booed up since I was 12 years old, I thought that was how a relationship flowed – break up to make up. The coolest times of those years were taking rides in his fast cars to hang out at the park. We often walked to the tennis court on the weekends to hit a couple of balls. Afterwards, we would stop at the corner grocery store for a pickle with a peppermint stick and a smokey joe on a homemade bun. The year that I lost my virginity to him; he gave me a promise ring. That diamond was so little that it could not be seen AT ALL. I was so proud of that ring because it meant all the arguments, slammed doors and fights were not being done in vain. It meant that we were committed to each other, no matter what, at least that's what I thought. Those years were spent with date nights at the movie, disco club, hotels, rides to Storm Creek and football games.

At the games when I would cheerlead, I couldn't concentrate because I was so consumed with who he was with and what he was doing. It was plenty of time to contemplate all of that since my schedule stayed booked and I always had a job (sometimes two). I didn't have to work and neither did he. The difference was that I wanted to. He didn't and would rather I didn't either.

As the relationship matured, so did the problems. During the many break-ups, I would date other boys. When my other relationships ended, I would go back to him. Sometimes the other guys would break up with me, because of news they'd receive that I was to forever belong to my "first love". Even with all the disconnects, there was obviously something that stuck because after high school, I enrolled during the summer and part of my freshmen year at the same university that he chose.

~Our Two Cents~

Our childhood is probably a shock to some of you and yet to others a milder version of your own life. As a child, we had to fight for our innocence and our physical safety. In doing so we learned to hide our pain.

One of us fought damn near every day of our young life because of the environment, social conditioning and for basic survival. In spite of all this, she remembers smiling a lot and being a happy kid. The other one struggled with being bullied and disliked for who she was, what she had and the status of her family, constantly attempting to be and do what everybody expected. There were a lot of children in the neighborhoods who probably had similar or worse stories than ours. That's not a badge of honor, but more so an admission of a failed society. It's society's duty and obligation to protect our most vulnerable: the poor, the handicapped, the elderly, the sick, and of course our precious gems – the children. There are all kinds of predators in our society and neighborhoods. The protection from them needs to be a collective effort.

The predators in our childhood were not just sexual, but also the bullies, the conditions of our neighborhoods, and ignoring and justifying unacceptable behavior because of their status and reputation.

SECTION TWO

Chapter 8 ~ Where to Next?

We took a short bus ride from Dallas to Houston, and arrived at night. I was in awe when I saw those city lights lit up against the buildings.

* * *

Before high school graduation, I needed to decide which college to attend. There was a lot of input from certain family members. I'd decided I was going to Indiana State to continue playing softball. Unfortunately, I was collectively told by the family that I was going to Bishop College in Dallas, Texas where my uncle had family. It was a cheap, all-black, Methodist school. It had been made abundantly clear that if my Aunt Jean, my mother's oldest sister, was going to help me, that is where I was going.

I started exploring other options like the military. I took the entrance exam and since I scored extremely well, I could join any branch I chose. I decided it would be the Navy. My mom was terribly upset, but I didn't care because I could go to school through the military. After I explained it to her, she was okay with the idea. The fact that I would be making a little money was a big selling point to her. My mind was made up until the Navy told me I would be going to boot camp in Florida and then to rating school in Great Lakes, Illinois. There was no way I was coming back to the Chicago area after eight weeks. I didn't care if it was Great Lakes.

By now Indiana State and other colleges were no longer an option so it was off to Bishop College. Having gone to a high school that was 99.9% African-American and living on the south side of Chicago, I could almost count on one hand the number of white people I'd had any interactions with. Going to Bishop was just like going to Wendell Phillips High School – no diversity.

I'd been struggling with the fact that Bishop was a smaller college and a demographic not much different from my high school. Even though I was performing well and making very good grades, I decided it might be best to transfer to another school for my degree in Business.

The decision to transfer from Bishop was a major moment in my life. I was making big girl moves. I knew I had to be prepared to make it work at all costs. Even though, while there, I'd made some lasting and genuine friendships, I felt I needed more. I hate to admit it now, but I thought graduating from Bishop College meant others would view my degree as less valuable because it would be from a small black, Methodist college. I devalued my heritage believing the education gained would be viewed as a joke by others. I don't regret my decision to transfer, but I do wish the decision process would have been more enlightened and not driven by fear.

Fear was always the main driving force of everything. Years of fear had manifested in every day of my existence – fear of not being loved, fear of Hank, fear of constant violence, fear of my brother, fear that Helen would be hurt, fear that I was not smart enough and the fear of not being accepted. You name it, I feared it.

Bishop had a lot of kids from Chicago, which was great for my adjustment to life away from home. We established a Chicago crew, hung out and was dedicated to protecting each other. I had a friend whose sister lived in Houston, Texas. A group of us decided to go for a visit the week of spring break. I was excited about the trip because this would give me an opportunity to visit the University of Houston, one of the schools I was considering for a transfer.

We took a short bus ride from Dallas to Houston. When we arrived at night, I was in awe when I saw those city lights lit up against the buildings. Even though I had grown up in Chicago most of my life, I'd never felt this way about the beauty of a city at night. This view of Houston was amazing, and I fell in love instantly. Dallas had not really grown on me, but Houston definitely had. Even though I loved the city of Houston and the University of Houston, I was born in Arkansas and had family there. So, I chose the University of

Central Arkansas (UCA), but Houston, Texas still captured my heart.

Chapter 9 ~ No "May" Flowers Here

When I woke in the morning, she was gone and left a note telling me to make sure to take everything I had there.

***

When I got to UCA, I was considered a sophomore, but having missed freshman orientation there was no bond shared with anyone. The only person I knew was my uncle who was a year and a half older than me. My roommate and I didn't really connect. There was a noticeable difference at UCA. I was aware of this prior to transferring, but still thought it was what I needed at that point in my life. Chicago had done a number on me. I was angry and needed to catch my breath. Even after attending school in Dallas for a year, I was still on the edge. I felt like I hadn't grown much as a person. Even worse than that, I didn't know if I needed to grow. I was just existing and surviving in Dallas. I felt like I was living an untrue life at Bishop. I never had any meaningful love interests and the school was a smaller version of Chicago.

The noticeable difference at UCA was there were white people everywhere. Of course, I'd seen white people before and had interacted with them when we'd come to Arkansas for the summer. However, while in Chicago, my interactions with them was nonexistent, unless it was an official encounter. I definitely didn't go to school with many, if any at all. I don't remember having a white classmate during my entire education in Chicago. UCA was so much different. We had to talk and interact every day with each other.

I was on a mission my first semester, so I kept to myself in the beginning. I wanted to get my GPA to a certain level so I could pledge Delta Sigma Theta Sorority, Inc. I was at a new school and wanted badly to fit in, but felt that had to wait until I pledged Delta. I had gone to all the mixers and made it clear I wanted to pledge, but they kept pushing back their acceptance and pledge period. My uncle was already established on the yard as an Omega man. When they finally decided to have a line, it was great news and perfect timing. I found myself in a bit of a situation when I befriended a young white girl. Her name was May. She was a little eccentric, but I found her charming. If they hadn't started a line when they did, my chances of getting in would've been slim.

I decided I wanted to be a Delta while in high school after doing a class report on Jewel LaFontaine. She was a prominent lawyer from Chicago who had worked in the Nixon Administration and was a Delta woman. She was such an accomplished and distinguished person. She had made it, so I wanted to take an interest in anything she had done. If pledging Delta Sigma Theta would help make me a successful woman, that's what I wanted.

My pledge period started. We were isolated and kept from everyone during this time. After making it through a very difficult, yet quick pledge period, I was now a Delta woman and felt a since of relief. I could now restart my friendship with the one person I had really connected with at UCA.

After pledging in 1983, I became too much of a wild card for the Delta's on the yard, so I decided I would move off campus. I felt like my personal life and activities were becoming an embarrassment for the sorority. These activities had started with drinking, smoking weed and hanging out with this very eccentric white girl. We would ride to Little Rock to just hang out and drink all day. When we talked, we never talked about boys, nor did we have any around us. I added nothing to this new friendship but grit and toughness and of course laughter. I never had any money and didn't have a car. I was basically riding her coat tail and free loading. I was living with my uncle for a minute, but most of the time I would spend the night over May's.

One day after spending the night with her, I needed to return to my uncle's apartment to get some things. When I got there, *that* girl was there. You know the one. The same girl that took my breath away when I was only thirteen years old. I came bursting in the door and she was sitting on the couch.

May was with me and she immediately noticed her beauty. I immediately broke into a smile and said, "What's up". She said hello in the most sophisticated tone.

She had such a presence about her. I felt the warmth inside of her coming through her voice. Those were the first words I had ever spoken to her. I introduced her to May and formally introduced myself. We'd never actually been introduced to each other. I knew about her, but didn't know if she knew about me. Why would she know anything about me? I introduced myself as the niece of her boyfriend's best friend. We told her we were going to the park to get high and asked if she wanted to come. She joined us and we talked and got high as hell, but later she had to return to the apartment.

When she left, May turned to me and said, "Wow! She is cute. Do you like her?" I didn't quite know what she meant by that question, but my response was, "Yes. She is cool and seems to be very nice." May said, "You know what I mean. Do you like her? You are gay right?" I was very high when I responded, so all I could get out was, "GAY? Oh, you mean like her like that?" I thought I was a having a tripping moment. I didn't think I was gay and how could May know that and not me and why would she ask me something like that? I had never been with a woman. May and I had never had sex, so what the hell was she talking about.

"How do you know I'm gay?" I asked. She said, "Well I thought you knew I was gay." She then stated she just thought I was taking it slow with her and said, "I must admit I was starting to think that maybe you weren't, but after seeing your whole body language change when Marilyn was around, I know you are now." Then she kissed me right on the mouth and well... I kissed her back. This was the first time I had ever kissed a girl. I kissed her with a feeling of comfortability and assurance. This kiss was also making me feel a certain kind of way.

We went back to her apartment that night and I didn't know what to do or how to do it. I thought back to how I felt with Chris and how every minute with him was about me. Everything came natural to me, the ease in which I felt everything I was doing was right. May's apartment was a room with an old lady living in the rest of the house. We had to be contained and quiet. She asked me afterward if I was lying about never being with a girl. I asked her why I would lie about that and she said she was just checking. This was something she wanted to do all the time and I was okay with it because I was enjoying myself. We had spent so much time together prior to that happening, but it never dawned on me we were working on a relationship because it didn't feel like that to me. I thought of her as a friend and a cool person to hang out with. I had seen and thought about much sexier girls at UCA, mostly black. She would drive me around, take me everywhere I needed to go and took exceptionally good care of me. It became apparent that she found my sex skills to be useful. I later realized she was paying me for my services. When I would mention a black girl's name even in the most innocent manner she would get visibly upset. Eventually, I became even more isolated from my sorority at school.

For the first time, someone was showing me all the attention and affection I wanted, and in a good way. I could not determine in my mind at the time if it was a perverted act. All my life, my church had taught me what I was now doing was the biggest sin anyone could commit. The acts engaged with May were worse than any other act ever committed, including the things that happened to me as a child. Other acts of cruelty committed by some were in no way worse than what I was doing.

Unfortunately, our relationship had started to become volatile at times. This made me nervous because all my life the only way I knew to resolve conflict was with physical confrontation. By this time, a part of me wondered if I was in love or in lust. I needed someone to want me, someone to love me, to need me, but I had nothing to offer her and she made that perfectly clear every time we got into an argument.

The words she would use to belittle me felt like punches from the playground of the Ickes. She had mastered the act of belittling me and making me feel like shit with words, but I had mastered the art of fighting and defending myself. I had perfected the skill of putting her in a position of fear. We were having these altercations regularly and it started getting old. The time had finally come for us to end the relationship, but not without one more final act of violence that led to me completely losing control.

Whenever we had these incidents, we'd make up and continue with this preposterous relationship. One night we decided to go to a club in Little Rock, just as friends. We were both free to engage in conversation with whomever we wanted to this night. Although I had been to this club many occasions, on this particular night the club was filled with beautiful black feminine women. I danced all night, which was and is still something I love to do. Dancing was one of the things that got me a lot of attention. I was an extremely good dancer. I had a natural way of catching every beat of a song. When I was little, my mama would ask me to dance for her friends. She would always manage to have a dance contest when all the kids were there, and I'd win every time, hands down.

This night in the club I danced and laughed with all these beautiful soulful sisters. We really enjoyed each other. There were no romantic flares, just a few smiles of interest. We settled down after spending so much time on the dance floor and found a spot where we all could talk. May joined us and we made it very clear on both our parts that we were not together. Everyone was enjoying each other's company. Then one of the young ladies said I danced very sexy. I was not used to recognizing when a girl was flirting with me. I could certainly tell when a guy was flirting, but never thought of a girl coming on to me. I thought her comments were complimentary and sweet. I told her that. She asked if I lived in the Rock. In the middle of telling her that I went to school in Conway, May yelled out, "And she has no car to come to visit either."

My face turned red as it could possibly turn. My eyes pierced toward her like a laser beam. It was like I was looking through her. I was angry and mad as hell. The other girls saw the look on my face. My mouth was clutched tightly, my eyes were seeing red, and it was obvious I was pissed. The ladies decided it was time to leave and I agreed as well. As we made our way to the exit doors, one of the girls asked if I was okay. I assured her I was fine. She immediately interrupted me to say, "No, I mean, are you really okay and not going to do anything foolish? That is a white girl; this is Arkansas. Don't be stupid because we can take you home."

I didn't want her to take me to Conway. I let her know that I was cool, but I knew inside I was not okay. This was the last time May would belittle me. When we hit the parking lot, she asked If I was good. "Hell no, I'm not good. You just embarrassed the shit out of me," I told her. She downplayed what I said and her response was, "Let's go!" When we got into the car, I asked her what her problem was. She went on this rant about how she had saved me from being embarrassed. Then she said with pride and conviction, "There's no way you would've been able to see her. You can't even drive this car if something was to happen to me right now." Then she slammed the brakes and pulled over and said, "Get out and drive."

I looked at her and said, "You really think I'm some kind of fool." I jumped out and walked over to the driver side. The car was a Ford Escort with a standard shift. I knew how to drive an automatic because I had taught myself from watching other people. The day I took my driver's license exam in high school, I had never driven a car. Studying every move my uncles, aunts and Helen made when they drove, I was basically self-taught.

At this point I knew she had no idea who I was. It didn't matter if I thought I was in love with her. She thought I was weak. When I made it to the driver's side, she was standing outside the car and I looked at her and said not a word. I jumped into the driver's seat. She hopped into the passenger side. I put my foot on the pedal, hit the clutch and she knew then that I could drive her car. Then anger and rage took over. I turned toward her and vehemently said, "I'm driving this car back to Conway tonight. When we get back there, I'm going to beat the shit out of you. If for some reason I don't get back tonight, I will beat your ass when I get there. I will hunt you down like a dog."

I had never felt so much rage in my life. This was the last time someone would walk over me. She was doing to me what so many others had done to me and I was done. She then grabbed the clutch and threw the car into first gear missing all the other gears. The car stopped almost immediately with a smell of smoke and transmission fuel. She screamed, "Get the hell out." I got out of the car and stood there by the driver's door. I told her that I planned on getting back into the car and going to Conway that night. I snatched the keys from the ignition switch. I held them up for her to see and then headed to the passenger's side.

She pushed me in my back and took a swing at me. I grabbed her by her neck and threw her up against the car with all my might. She started screaming and I felt myself losing control of my thoughts. She was struggling to get her breath when a car pulled up and asked if she was okay. My back was toward the car and she was still struggling. She looked into my eyes and suddenly her face reappeared. I snapped out of what had taken over me and saw the fear in her eyes. As tears ran down my face, I loosened my grip on her neck. She then waved off the people in the car and told them that she was fine.

She told me to get in the car. I kept the keys until we got in. When I gave her the keys, we rode back without saying one word to each other. She just stared at the road. I looked straight ahead with tears in my eyes. I don't know what happened to me in that moment. I was at a total loss for words. All I wanted to do at that moment was squeeze out of her neck all the pain I had ever felt in my life. I was filled with sorrow and shame that she had made me do something so evil. All these thoughts were going through my mind.

She had kept me from my sorority and from my friends. I was engulfed in anger. I wanted to blame her for my behavior. She had made me this person. We made it back to Conway late into the morning and she asked me to stay at her place. I stayed the night and we both went to sleep like nothing had happened. We did not speak at all about the incident. There was no discussion – it was in the bed and off to sleep.

When I woke in the morning, she was gone and had left a note telling me to make sure to take everything I had there. She lived a few blocks from my uncle's place, making for an exceptionally long walk back home. I knew I had to apologize for my behavior. I was not expecting to continue our relationship, but I had to make right what I had done. When I got to my uncle's apartment, I was taking a bath and heard a knock at the door. I could hear the voice of authority ask for me by name. When I came around the corner toward the front door, there was a sheriff with a piece of paper in his hand. He came to serve me with a restraining order, demanding that I stay at least 300 feet away from May.

He asked me to step outside and he then carefully explained exactly what it all meant. If I was to break this order, I could find myself in a lot of trouble. I could see his lips moving and I could hear him, but surely he was not serious. In my naiveté and stupid frame of mind I thought I could at least apologize. After a couple of attempts, May went back to the sheriff's department and reported that I had violated the restraining order.

Even though May and I came from totally different backgrounds we had formed a friendship. I had been to her house in Jonesboro, met her family and spent the night with them. She had even been to my grandmother's house in Helena. Since my arrival at UCA, I had not really formed any other friendships. With our relationship ending and now facing an upcoming court date, this was a low and lonely time for me.

There was no physical battle for me to fight this time. I wished it were one because that is something that I did well. Now I was faced with fighting an emotional battle – something I had never done in my life. I had no idea how to deal with my emotions. I had hidden them for so long. All the things that happened to me, I'd been hell bent on not letting them be an excuse for me to fail. If I never talked about them or gave them breath, I would have no reason to fail. I was fearful of my pain becoming a clutch for any failure in my life. I never wanted to be a victim of my hurt.

I had sunken into a very deep hole of darkness. I felt worthless. I was fearful of having to face my family. I had embarrassed everyone that knew me and cared about me – my uncle, his friends and my sorority. I spent days depressed laying in the bed. One day I decided I would just end it all. I tried with everything in me to harm myself, but I was not successful. I guess that angel the doctor mentioned to me in high school while lying in the emergency room had manifested again. Only this time it intervened in the form of an Omega man. He stopped me from breaking my mama and sister's heart that day.

After that incident, the family thought it would be best if I went home to my grandmother's house to wait on my court date. There was not much conversation about what happened on the ride home. I guess everyone was waiting for me to speak with my mother, Helen, before they spoke to me. She called me when I made it to the house. She asked me what was going on and I started to cry. The words could not come out of my mouth. I never answered her. I just cried like a baby over the phone. She then asked loudly, "Are you gay?"

When I didn't answer again, she said, "Listen to me. I don't give a damn what you are. You don't have to answer me. I just want you to know something. I don't care who you fuck, I just want you to handle yourself with class. Don't let any bitch ever make you act like that again. Do you understand?" She then said, "I need you to answer that one," and I said, "Yes ma'am." She then said for the first time in my life without me saying it first, "I love you. Now put your aunt back on the phone." I wiped the tears from my face and handed my aunt the phone. After that phone call, there was not much conversation in my grandmother's house about that incident or my sexuality... well at least not around me.

The only thing left now was the court date for the violation of my restraining order. During this period, I spent much more time with my Aunt Heavenly. She had just started her family and had two young kids. I started hanging around her a lot to help out and spend time with them. They gave me a peace of mind when I was around them.

One day when I went to visit, *she* was there. You know who… Marilyn. She had to have heard what happened with me and May. I was so embarrassed, so I spoke in a low and timid voice. She responded in the biggest and boldest voice I had ever heard, "Hey there. How are you doing," with a big, beautiful smile. I could feel her energy and that warm, caring spirit flowing through her voice as if she wanted to tell me that everything would be okay.

I still felt a rush of excitement whenever I was in her presence. I could not let those emotions creep into my mind, especially since I had just embarrassed my entire family. I thought the thing with May had to be a phase, so I couldn't understand this feeling I had every time I saw Marilyn. It seemed like every time I'd go to my aunt's house she would be there. This was no surprise since my aunt was my uncle's sister… yeah, the uncle who was Marilyn's boyfriend's best friend. I barely spoke to her, barely holding my head up most of the time.

She finally asked one day if I was okay. I told her I was fine. She said, "If you ever want to talk let me know. I'm here." My aunt had been trying all summer to get me to feel good about myself. She would listen to me all day and night, going up and down emotionally. She was glad to see me respond to someone else besides her and her husband, Uncle Calvin.

One day I decided I'd finally ask Marilyn to talk because I could only tell my aunt and uncle so much. I needed someone to hear my side, my thoughts. She responded with a yes and a smile. I started telling her everything that had happened from my version with my real emotions. I talked so much before I knew it, I had fallen into a level of comfortability that I had never felt before. It seemed like I would never stop talking, but she sat there and listened to every word. I could see tears forming in her eyes. When I finally finished, she said, "Well, you know what? It's not the end of the world and you will bounce back."

Then she reached across the table and grabbed me by the hand and pulled me closer to her and I felt an instant warmth go through my body. I looked up at her with tears running down my face because I had shared my entire story with my head down in shame. She looked me right in my face and told me the only thing I did wrong was put my hands on her. If I loved her and she did not want me or love me back, then I should have walked away. She said, "I know you feel bad, but you have not done anything that can't be fixed. You tried to make it right."

She asked if I had been praying. I looked at her with a face of confusion. How could I pray about this situation since I had committed the biggest sin of all? I told her I had not. I guess she could sense I was uncomfortable talking about that. She then said, "That's okay. I will pray for you." Then out of nowhere she said, "You are smart; start using your brain. Communicate with your words and stop reacting with your emotions." Then she reached across the table, wiped the tears from my face and said, "And please smile more. Everything will be fine."

I started crying uncontrollably and shaking. I thought I was going to pass out. My heart was hurting so bad, but not just because of what I had done to May. I felt so much shame and guilt for my family and I thought there was no way I'd ever be looked at the same way again. I had spent all my life moving around in this family as almost invisible. Now when I was finally seen it was to bring shame and embarrassment to them. I was now officially the black sheep of the family.

She held my hand the whole time I was shaking and crying. I kept my head down and when I finally looked up, she had her eyes closed and she was moving her lips, muttering something. Then I realized she was praying for me. She was asking the Lord to help me, to come into my life and put his arms around me.

~MJ's Journey~

> When Wilma told me she had to go to court for assaulting May, I had so many thoughts. At first I thought May had lied, but when Wilma told the whole story, I was like, "WOW! How did she allow that girl to take her

there?" When she told me the breakdown of the incident, I kept thinking of the first time I met them together at her uncle's house and then going to the park. Things felt a little off, but never in the sense that it would get violent.

Whatever had taken place, I knew Wilma sincerely felt awful. I wanted her to know that doing a bad act didn't make one a bad person. I wanted to share with her what always freed me from bad decisions and that was prayer. So yeah, I grabbed her hand and began to pray. I prayed and asked God to give her the strength to endure the repercussions of what was to come legally, but also from the family and from May.

That was the day my heart started to mend. I gathered my composure and realized I could and would make it, but there was still a court date and I would need to speak before a judge. I had to convince these people that I was not a danger to May or anyone. But how was I going to do that if I couldn't control my anger or communicate my feelings effectively.

Marilyn said, "Let us practice on your court day." Because she had a way with words and creative writing skills, she wrote what I needed to say. She was emphatic about how I was to say things and present myself. So, that's what we did everyday – practiced. As time was approaching, she kept asking if I was okay. Every day she encouraged me that I could do this. Then she said, "How about we work on softening your look?"

Softening my look? What the heck did that mean? She said, "Maybe some make-up and a little lipstick to bring out your smile." It was a few days before court and I told her I wished she could come with me. She instantly said, "I can go if you want me to." My face lit up. "Great! I will let my aunt and grandmother know." I told them she wanted to go and they quickly responded by saying she was only trying to get a ride up there to see her boyfriend. That was fine because I just wanted her there with me so I could get through this mess.

The day had finally come. Marilyn, my grandmother, Aunt Jean and I were on our way to court so I could defend myself against harassment charges. It was a very long and quiet ride to Conway. When we got to court, my case was called. I was informed that my restraining order had been pulled and dropped. May had dropped the restraining order and didn't want to pursue the matter any further. She didn't even come to court that day.

I hugged my grandmother and aunt, and then ran over to Marilyn and gave her the biggest hug with a smile. She said, "I told you It would be okay." As we headed to the car to go back to Helena, I asked her if she wanted to go see her boyfriend. She turned to me and I could see she wanted to. I asked my aunt if we could go by the apartment so I could get some things. I wanted her to see him because if that was what she wanted, whatever made her happy would make me happy.

From that moment on, I knew I would do whatever made her smile. Marilyn and I had developed a deep bond and our friendship was cemented that summer. We both realized that we genuinely cared about each other's well-being. We were on the threshold of an amazing friendship. I think we both felt that way and knew the importance of this relationship. We knew we had to approach it with caution and respect.

Friendship had always been the cornerstone of my growth. I had learned to place friendships in a vault, reminding me to always be loyal to those that were there for me in my darkest and scariest moments. My friend from high school, Vanessa, returned to help me when others didn't care. My mother had been my friend the day when I was at my lowest and most confusing moment. She knew I would respond if she challenged me to be better than my circumstances and to focus on the reality in front of me. It was the same way I responded when I took that beating from Felicia and she challenged me to never let anyone hurt me and get away with it.

For this particular incident, she challenged her baby girl to hold on in 'Helen-style' – cussing. I knew she had also faced challenges with anger where she too would lose control. She wanted better for me and she needed for me to find a way to hold on. She didn't know what to say or how to tell me, but knew that I had to.

Marilyn had spent the entire summer building me up and getting me ready to return to UCA with a spark. She saw I was lost, but she also saw that I was not defeated with so much more to give. She got to see the funny and witty side of me. I would tell her funny stories and she had this contagious laughter that was followed by tears. I asked her why she cried when she laughed. She said they were happy tears.

I shared things from my childhood that I was comfortable talking about at the time. It felt like I was sharing everything with her, but she wasn't sharing anything with me. Maybe she was keeping a secret like I was. Even though she was a sweet and caring girl, there was a shield there. She would not let me go beyond that shield. That was okay with me because I was glad that she made me smile again.

We also worked on re-branding me. We felt after the trial that I needed to be ready for the after effects of my debacle of a relationship with May. This would be the last time I would use the 'Wilma' part of my name. I would go only by Naomi Wilma now. My full name is Naomi Wilma Jean Scales. Many people didn't know my name was Naomi in high school, but this would be the summer that Wilma from

Chicago died and Naomi was born.

Chapter 10 ~ A Little Bit of This, A Little Bit of That

"Stop! Stop! Stop! He is not worth it. I got it. Please stop." She was so scared... He ran to the other side of the laundry room fearful for his life yelling, "Get that Bitch! What the fuck is wrong with her?" My aunt burst through the laundry door with a hunter's knife in her hand...

* * *

Upon my return to UCA in the Fall of '84, I immediately took a full load of classes to get back to the books so that I could graduate on time. I got back involved with the sorority on a regular. I got a job and things were looking good. I was not interested in dating. I just wanted to readjust to being a part of the college experience. I wasn't sure if people were trying to date me to see if I was straight or gay. I mainly hung with the sorors and our new pledgees' line for the fall.

Marilyn was back and it was great knowing I had her with me. She had told me during the summer she was thinking about coming back. She never shared much about the things that led to her leaving. She would only share that she had a really hard time in Atlanta and because of the circumstances she finished the final few hours that were left and merged her transfer hours.

She became involved with the sorors and we started spending quite a bit of time together, but she wanted me to get back on the horse and start dating again. When she wasn't with the sorors, she was spending time with her boyfriend. Whenever she got the chance, she would inquire about my love life. She kept asking if I was going to start dating someone or at least "get some". When she said, "get some", she never referred to a man or woman. She just wanted me to be in the company of someone.

Marilyn would constantly say that I was too cool and amazing not to be with someone that could appreciate my personality. Whenever she spoke, it was the way she put her words together. I realized just why she had a journalism scholarship. I told her I wasn't sure if I wanted to date anyone. I wasn't sure if I would drift back into my promiscuous ways from Bishop when it came to men. Then I wasn't sure if I wanted to take a chance with a girl because of what had just happened.

She started sharing a little snippet about her relationship with her boyfriend. I knew something was going on because she started being seen with other guys and *then* there was the incident at the apartments.

When we'd returned to school for the fall, my Aunt Heavenly had also decided to go back to complete her degree. She had attended UCA as well in the late 70's, but left. I was living with her, her kids and an elderly cousin in a large apartment. I was working as a receptionist at a roofing company around a lot of dirty old men. It was good pay when he paid. Marilyn was living with her boyfriend downstairs a few apartments over from our place and we saw each other quite a bit.

I knew about this guy she was spending time with when she and her boyfriend were on bad terms. Her boyfriend would go for days staying at other women's places and she wasn't sitting around waiting on him. They were on and off a lot during this time. This was one of the times when they were back on, so she had to tell this guy to chill. This guy knew what he was getting into and fully understood what was going on, but he didn't want to play along anymore.

He didn't take it well this time and he started stalking her. This day he had cornered her in the laundromat of the apartment complex. I was in the apartment talking with my Aunt Heavenly and cousin when one of the kids came running into the apartment yelling, "Some man has Marilyn blocked in the laundry room." I grabbed my cousin's bat from his room and started running toward the laundry room. Aunt Heavenly told her son to stay with our cousin and his baby sister in the apartment. This was the same aunt who had come to visit my mom in Chicago when the Hank fight occurred. She knew what was going on and was battle tested and ready.

When I entered the laundry room, Marilyn was backed into a corner with a clothes hanger in her hand yelling, "I told you we had to call it quits." His eyes were red and his face was darker than normal because his blood was boiling.

I rushed in without a second thought and swung the bat barely missing his head. He looked at me with the fear of death in his eyes. Marilyn screamed to the top of her lungs and it echoed throughout the laundry room like a wounded soul full of fear. "Stop! Stop! Stop! He is not worth it. I got it. Please stop." She was so scared because she didn't know if I would kill him or not. He ran to the other side of the laundry room fearful for his life yelling, "Get that Bitch! What the fuck is wrong with her?"

My aunt burst through the laundry door with a hunter's knife in her hand, saw me drooling from the mouth and Marilyn crying saying, "Get her. I got this." My aunt called my name and I snapped out of it and I could see them all clearly now. The adrenaline had been flowing fast, but my heart was starting to slow down. He said, "I'm leaving. We good. I won't fuck with you again." I don't remember saying a word. All I remember is that she was in danger. I didn't need to know what… only that she was in danger. There was no way I was going to let anyone harm her… anyone. After that incident, she didn't share as much with me about her boyfriend, especially things that brought her pain.

After things had settled, she wanted to talk to me again about getting back on the horse. This time she was sure it had to be a woman. She was convinced of this more than me. She told me she wanted me to meet someone. I'm thinking to myself, 'Okay. What kind of guy is this,' and then she said a girl's name. "A Girl?" I asked with a perplexed voice. "You know what happened the last time I tried that." I decided I would be content with dating guys because it kept my emotions intact. I basically had no emotions for men – not the kind that a woman could bring out in me. If being with a man would keep my emotions under control, it would be men I would date until I got the heck out of this school.

I was so scared of being with a woman because I wasn't sure if I could control my passion and fire that burned inside when I was with a girl. I didn't say out loud what I was thinking, but to myself it was, 'What the hell is she doing?' I was beyond furious with her when she approached me with that crap. What the hell was she trying to do? We had just spent the whole summer putting me back together. I knew I had to respond in a manner that was not threatening to her. I didn't want to scare her, and I sure didn't want to come off aggressive.

She said, "Listen to me. You need to know if it was a phase and if you can control yourself. You know people do that kind of stuff all the time." I asked, "What kind of stuff?" She said,

"Kiss a girl, touch a girl… all kinds of stuff. But that does not make you gay." I was really confused now. What kind of crazy stuff is she talking? I looked at her with a baffled face and asked, "What does it make you if it isn't gay?" She looked me directly in my face and said, "Stop getting caught up about the sex part." She then went on to say, "That girl did a number on you and maybe it was the mental games you couldn't handle. If you like girls, that's cool but you must find out. I don't want you to think something is wrong with you because you can't handle your emotions."

Was she challenging me to rise to the occasion? Yes, she was and I was aroused by her approach. I trusted her and felt she was doing what she thought was best for me. I believed she had my best interest at heart. I said I'd meet her so she set it up. It was someone she knew who liked both males and females. She was a good girl on the surface to the public, but liked being with girls undercover.

This was a time period when people just didn't run around saying they were bisexual or homosexual. This was before the rainbow, openness and being fluid. Homosexuality was a big taboo, especially in the south and among black people. So that made it a double taboo. This was the era when everything was on the down low.

I had spent the whole summer before thinking I was weird

and dirty because this was something other black people didn't do. Now she's telling me this kind of stuff happens all the time, even among black people. I was so freaking naïve. There were a lot of things going on even at Bishop, but it wasn't this kind of stuff. Everyone was straight at Bishop, or at least I thought so.

I went to the dorm room to meet Marilyn's friend so we could study together. But hell, I don't think we even had a class together. She was light skinned, extremely cute, but not as beautiful as Marilyn. She didn't have that silky bronze brown skin and long beautiful black hair. I was still intrigued because she was very attractive. I told her who I was and that I was a friend of Marilyn's. She smiled and said, "You're cute."

We talked about school and all the people we both knew. As we sat on the edge of her bed, I could sense we were done with the small talk, so I kissed her. She returned the kiss very passionately. This led to a good twenty minutes of kissing and exploring. We enjoyed each other, but we didn't go all the way because her roommate returned. When it was time to leave, I let her know that I had really enjoyed myself and that I would like to see her again.

I left that night feeling good about myself. I had passion and desire. I felt in control and I did like her, but I could move on if I had to without any trepidation. I could tell she liked me also and wanted to see me again, but this time I would control the tempo of this friendship. I would make it clear that this would be just a friendship. I was not going to spend the night or be seen in public together. This would be exactly what we both wanted – a friend with benefits type of relationship. We both respected each other's wishes.

I saw Marilyn a few days after that and she wanted to know how the date went. I told her it went well without giving many details. She wanted the details, but I would not share them with her. For some strange reason I didn't want her to know how much I had enjoyed being with her friend. I didn't want her to feel a certain kind of way. She had actually already spoken to her friend and got her version of the night. She told Marilyn she was looking forward to sleeping with me and it would have happened that night if her roommate had not come back. She also shared that I was a fine ass girl and very passionate.

Marilyn tried all that afternoon to get me to share, but I wouldn't. I was very vague with my responses to her. She wanted to get something to eat so I suggested we go to Hardees. When we got there, she put me in a head lock to make me tell her about the night. We were laughing and playing around. Then she tightened her grip pulling my face up against her breast. I could smell her body scent; it was tantalizing.

We met eye to eye as I tried to get loose from her grip. I didn't want to move, but I knew I had to because I was beginning to feel too comfortable nestled against her chest. It felt like I was meant to be there. She quickly let my neck go as we approached the door and then asked if I was hungry. I yelped an excited yes, I was obviously on cloud nine as she looked at me with a huge grin. I could see that dimple on her right cheek with her snarky smile. "I just bet you are." She said those words in a sinister type voice. I felt like she was coming on to me, but I had to check myself. I sensed I was at the intersection of desperation and stupidity.

~MJ's Journey~

I was very curious about what I felt and thought when I was around Wilma. When we were at Hardees, yes, I was flirty and very touchy feely with her. I felt comfortable doing that, but didn't know what to do with it beyond that and decided that I was "just being flirty", nothing more and nothing less. It was just like I had done in the past, but this time felt different. We always laughed a lot when we were together, but this day felt excessively extra. I enjoyed myself and did not want it to end. For the first time I felt this could be different and that different is okay but wrong is not, so I dismissed it.

I finally came to the realization that girls were coming on to me, some were open and obviously flirting. All the other times I guess I didn't have the confidence to recognize it. Not to mention Marilyn was every bit of a straight girl since she had a boyfriend – a boyfriend I knew very well. I had to be wrong about this one. She had never indicated anything else to me. I had to get a grip. I then lightly pushed her in the back playfully and said, "I hope you got some money," as we entered the door of Hardees.

Since being back on the yard and active with the sorority again, we knew I was red meat for other sororities, especially with the upcoming Greek show. It was all over campus what had gone on with me and the white girl. Everyone pretty much knew about each other's business, whether good or bad.

The Greek show was a big deal where all the sororities and fraternities would step on the yard during homecoming weekend. At this time during the early 80's, each Greek organization would go hard at each other. If there was spice or juice that could be used to attack, it was fair game. We needed to come up with a routine to offset the shade that would be thrown my way. We pondered and pondered and decided we would only make one shade statement about a rival sorority, and instead focus on our sisterhood. I and one of the sorors wrote a tune to a popular Billy Ocean song, *Caribbean Queen*, to show our love for DST.

We were a hit on the yard, but I was dealt my fair amount of shade. Oldhead sorors returned to the yard for the show. They were very impressed with our show of unity. It wasn't like all the sorors didn't know about my troubles, and I'm sure some of them really didn't care for me, but it was too late for that now. I was a soror and they were not going to let me get blasted on the yard without some push back.

Winter of '84, we were back in Helena. We would usually go hang out at my Aunt Heavenly's house. She had left Conway and returned to Helena. We'd had somewhat of a falling out because during the time we were roommates, I was responsible for my portion of the apartment rent, which was one room in a four-bedroom apartment. I was paying half of the entire monthly rent. I had a job, but, hell, half the time my boss was not paying me on time and when he did it was just a portion of my check. Most of the time I would never have my entire part of the rent when it was due on the first of the month. I would take my aunt's part and tell her I would pay the rent, but I always needed more time. I would not pay it on time and would lie like I had. Late charges started to accumulate and then came the eviction notice.

The late charges added to almost a full month amount of rent. They repeatedly demanded their money. When we received the eviction notice, my aunt was devastated. She could not believe we owed so much in late fees. I was ashamed, and acted like they made a mistake, but there was no mistake. Here I go again. Now I was adding *liar* to all my other acts of less than stellar behavior.

My aunt had decided she'd had enough of school and would go back home. She would not be returning after the Christmas break. Even though there were other factors that contributed to her return home, I felt like I was most at fault. I had to make it right with my aunt. I had to get some money from that asshole of a boss of mine to take care of the late fees.

I spent hours in the office with these rednecks who would make all kinds of racial, insensitive, and inappropriate comments throughout the day about my ass. The boss man would occasionally give me a shoulder massage and always handled our employer/employee relationship inappropriately but I was determined to get my money. I had asked and begged enough.

I had survived to this point making my own decisions. Even though I'd made some mistakes I was alive, unlike so many from my hood and the projects. My instincts and actions had gotten me this far. I was only 20, but it felt like I had lived much longer, especially considering all the stuff I had seen and been involved in. Hell, I had survived a stabbing in high school and a robbery at gunpoint while working when attending Bishop College. I wasn't too afraid of many things at this point. I was never nervous about doing anything from a physical standpoint. I was a tomboy growing up so physical challenges I welcomed. However, I went to Marilyn before I did something that would reflect badly on my upbringing and bring more light to my anger problems.

The roofing company office had a lot of expensive items, in particular, an antique clock that was a beautiful piece of artwork. My 20-year old mind and over-the-top imagination crafted this brilliant idea to take a few of those items for myself so that I could pawn them to get the money I needed. As college students, we had learned the act of pawning things. When I needed money to prove to May that I wasn't a total loser, I would pawn things to get some quick cash. I was going to steal the items from the office and pawn them back home instead of the local pawn shop.

When I presented the idea to Marilyn, she asked me if I was crazy, and then she said, "Plus you will get caught." My crazy idea seemed to be something that made her excited, almost like an aphrodisiac. I was expecting an immediate *hell no*, but she wanted to hear my plan.

After explaining my plan to her she quickly said, "You need someone to look out for you. I will go with you and be your lookout," and then she started running off all this other stuff I needed to make sure were taken care of before I left the office. It was like she was experienced at this. I'm thinking to myself; she does have a dark side.

We waited until the office closed and a few hours before sunset. We didn't want to drive out there in the dark with our hearts racing and nervous. We were afraid and didn't want to make a mistake. She was smart and had everything planned to the tee. We made our initial drive by the office to make sure it was clear. Then she dropped me off a few hundred feet past the office. I walked back toward the office where there was a narrow pathway through a lightly wooded area. I climbed through the front window because I knew it did not lock.

I had a trash bag tucked away in my pants. I was very athletic and still a bit of a tom boy and damn near jumped straight up and through the window. I grabbed that clock. I didn't know how much it was worth, but it had to be worth something. I grabbed a few other little items. I had to make sure not to be seen coming out the window with a trash bag. I took the bag to the back of the building and put it outside by the back door before I jumped through the window. We had discussed that if someone was coming down the road, she would signal by flashing the lights. If anyone was to come up to her and ask questions, she was to get out of the car and pretend she had car problems. I had to make sure I put everything back in the right place and wiped everything down.

As I started to jump out the window, she flashed the lights over and over. I knew that meant someone was coming down the road, but why was she flashing so many times? I immediately darted back into the office. It was becoming too busy to go out the front window. Time had passed and people who lived close to the office were coming home from work. We had worried about the night fall, but forgot about commuters coming from work seeing us. This meant I had to leave out the back door.

This was a door that required a key to lock. I thought about it and said to myself, 'What the hell? They saw me leave from work earlier today and it was through this same door.' I thought if no one saw me leave earlier they would automatically assume I was the one that left the door unlocked. Luckily, everyone had seen me leave before the last person left that night. That meant someone other than me had to leave the door unlock. I did my last wipe down of everything I touched and headed out the back where I'd placed the bag outside.

It suddenly dawned on me that we used a portable step during the daytime for everyone to enter this particular door. I opened the door to step onto the first step and fell face down onto the grass. I was in tremendous pain. I couldn't scream. I felt like I had fallen from a five-story building and started to freak out. I was hoping I had not broken my ankle. Part of our plan was making sure I showed up to work the next day. That meant I couldn't come in all scarred up or limping.

I was able to get up from the ground and close the door, but the pain started to feel unbearable. I made my way through the woods back to the spot. It took me a little longer than planned because I was in severe pain. Marilyn wasn't there when I got there and I was hoping she hadn't gone looking for me in the building because I wasn't there at the anticipated time we had calculated. My legs were stinging from the pain. Felt like I had definitely broken something.

Finally, she pulled up to the spot. I was so excited to see her. There was a dumpster nearby from an apartment complex. She grabbed a bag of trash out of the trunk of her car and walked toward the dumpster and there I was looking like a wounded dog barely able to move. She went to get the car to pull it closer and to allow the trunk to obstruct the view. She then grabbed another bag of trash from the car. That's when I slowly stood up with my trash bag to make it look like I was putting it in the dumpster, but instead I threw it into the trunk.

I got in on the passenger side of the car. She got in the car and looked at me and we both burst out laughing. I looked at her and started laughing so hard I was about to piss in my pants. I told her, "I can't believe I just did that." She said, "Yes, you did, and I can't believe I helped you." We laughed so hard. With excitement, I screamed, "I got that damn clock as well." She then said, "I knew it was going to work." I'm thinking how in the world did she know for sure that this crazy plan would work.

I had to ask her why was she so sure it would work. Looking me squarely in the eyes, without a smile or grin, she said; "Because when we were working on the plan you had one mission. That was to make everything right with your aunt and you went through every possible situation in your mind." She then said, "You were determined not to fail." I looked at her and said, "You damn right about that. I will not have them (family) talking about my ass behind my back about this shit and the money I owe her."

We went to the liquor store to get some E&J Brandy and then to get some food. When we made it back to the apartment, we left everything in the trunk. We were meeting some other sorors that evening as part of the planned alibi story. I took a few Tylenol pills, cleaned myself up and off to party with the sorors.

The next day I went to work like nothing had happened. They didn't notice much at first, but as the day went on someone noticed the clock was missing. It was a big fuss and everyone was freaking out, but there wasn't anyone to blame. My first thought is that someone else knew that the front window didn't lock. However, because the back door was unlocked it was now time to figure out who had left last. I was cleared because everyone had seen me leave earlier that day.

Marilyn and I had pulled it off. This would be the first of many secrets we would share between us. This created an even more powerful bond because we now had a secret. We were inseparable physically and emotionally and had connected on another level of devious curiosity.

We were home for spring break, and I could give my aunt some of the money I owed her. She told me I didn't have to give her anything, but I told her I felt guilty about her having to leave school. She told me that it wasn't my fault, but I felt like it was. Marilyn had come over to play cards one afternoon. My aunt had to make a few runs before the card game started, so we fixed a couple of drinks and sat on the couch. We started talking about the office break-in and that girl from school came up again. This time Marilyn was hell bent on getting some real facts. I asked why she wanted to know. She said, "Hell, I don't know why, but it's been on my mind since the hook up." I asked her jokingly if she was jealous, and she replied that she didn't know.

I looked at her with confusion. I was thinking to myself not to do something or say something stupid at this moment. I was convinced she meant that if she was jealous it was more like envy of the friendship. I decided to make a joke of the conversation, a trait that had come in handy throughout my life. I had learned to use comedy to avoid tough and difficult conversations. I told her a lame joke about how I could not tell her because she would be cock blocking.

I looked at her and she had a look on her face that melted my heart. She was looking perplexed and a little sad and I didn't want to hurt her feelings. I had to fix it. I gently grabbed her by the chin and turned her head towards me and I told her I was just playing. I didn't like the other girl like that and that I just was messing with her. I reminded her I had been concentrating on school because my GPA had dropped since my pledge period and the following semester during the time of dealing with the May nightmare. I told her I didn't have time for that right now.

She looked at me with a gleam in her eyes and a smile and softly said, "Okay." When my aunt walked through the door, we were face to face, staring each other in the eyes. My aunt said nothing, but she could feel there was some tension in the room. She asked if we were ready to start playing cards. We played cards all night and laughed as usual. The time approached for us to end the night, but I needed a ride back to my grandmother's house. My aunt was going to take me, but Marilyn said she would give me a ride. I thought that was cool, hoping maybe she had some weed to smoke on the way.

We got in the car and I asked where the weed was. She looked at me and said, "You know I want to kiss you so bad right now." My only reaction was to put my hand on my chin. I was looking like someone had asked me what the meaning of life was. I told her, "You know we can't, right?" This was confirmation of my feelings from earlier in the night. Her questions about Cassie were a real warning to shield her from the pain of that night. I could not let my guard down because we could not be in this position. Her boyfriend was damn near family.

I simply stated she didn't have to say that to me to be nice and I knew she was trying to make me feel good about myself. I figured if I spoke from a platonic point of view, we would not have to talk about it even though she had made it clear she could kiss me. We both knew that was clearly a no. She repeated it and started naming the reasons why. She said I was kind, strong, and had quite a sense of humor and she really enjoyed being around me and laughter was also a big part of our friendship.

I had never felt so comfortable being around someone as I did with her. I was starting to feel like myself again, starting to live in my true spirit. My smile was constantly on display when we were together. I was hoping that this conversation wouldn't make her feel different or embarrassed the next day.

I wanted to lighten the atmosphere in the car, so once again I made a joke out of the conversation, to let her know that I was still cool even if she made a mistake telling me that. I told her, although she wanted to kiss me, she couldn't because I would then have to stalk her and we both started laughing. I said, "On a serious note, we can't do that, but for the record, I wanted to kiss you as well."

Then she went full sorority sister on me and said, "You know I care about you soror, right?" I guess that was her way of speaking from a platonic point of view as well. I was not going to be the weakest link in the conversation; I couldn't get emotional. I had to maintain my emotions and show her I had improved my head game since my ordeal with May. I was not going to mess this up and I wasn't sure if I was completely fixed from my previous behavior.

As cool as I could be while trying my best to hide the fact that my heart had just skipped a beat, I said, "Now do you have any weed?" She said yes, but we had to smoke it on the way because she was meeting him. I got home and I could hear my heart beating. My hands were sweating, and I thought about her all night. The next day, my Aunt Heavenly came by my grandmother's house to visit and before she left, she wanted to ask me something. She wanted to know if anything was going on between myself and Marilyn. I quickly assured her that nothing was going on making sure she understood that nothing could happen between me and Marilyn. I also needed to make it crystal clear to her that what happened with May was just a phase in my life. She seemed satisfied with my answer, but before she left, she turned around and said, "I just wanted to make sure because you all need to stop it now if it is."

Marilyn came by my grandmother's house later the same day, which assured me she was okay with everything from our conversation on the previous night. We started talking business as usual. We both seemed anxious, pre-occupied with our thoughts, and couldn't take being around each other much that day. It was getting harder and harder for us to part ways from each other the more time we spent together. Something was going on here and that was the last thing we needed. I had this feeling as if something was bubbling in my stomach when she came around. I could not maintain my enthusiasm when she was near me. There was an instant grin on my face whenever she would appear. Surely this could not be happening.

~MJ's Journey~

Although I kept quizzing Wilma about her date with Cassie, I am not sure why I wanted to know the answers to what I was asking. I wanted their hook up to work out but I didn't want it to last. These times spent with Wilma were so much fun. She made me laugh and kept me entertained. I enjoyed being with her but I started to notice that I began to feel different when I was around her. Our times together began to become awkward. It seemed as though I needed to do some self-assessment and soul searching. My feelings, conversations and thoughts regarding Wilma began to be out of sync with the norm. I didn't want our times together or conversations to end. Even our phone conversations would tickle my fancy. I dismissed it to being curious. I'm not sure what I was curious about since I didn't think curiosity could cause stomach butterflies, twinkling eyes and possibly even LIES.

I kept telling myself she was just queer curious. Hell, I thought I was just queer curious. Wasn't I? Now I was starting to feel an emotion I had never felt before. I had loved Chris, but this emotion was much stronger. It felt like she was oxygen and I needed her to breathe. What the hell was happening? I needed to see her every day and she felt the same way. Oh Boy!

Chapter 11 ~ Not Quite the Suga Daddy

But here I was again in another hot mess. Just like with May, I had turned over my independence and willingness to do for myself to someone because they had shown a slight capability of taking care of my material needs... the only person I knew to call was her.

* * *

There is an old saying that if you love something set it free. If it's meant to be it will come back to you.

When I returned to school the spring of '85, Marilyn and I had both decided we would try not to spend too much time together. Also, I felt I needed to take a serious attempt at the dating scene again. I was determined I would only date men. After the spring break incident with Marilyn I didn't want to bring confusion into our friendship. Marilyn had a boyfriend and she needed to work on her relationship. I was not naïve to the fact that the statement about the kiss from Marilyn warranted more attention, but I wasn't interested in going down that road. I knew I had an enormous crush on her, but protecting her soul and spirit was the most important thing to me in the world. Having her in my life was worth any personal sacrifices.

I had finally gotten to a point where I was driving, working, and functioning as a real adult. I had a few dates, but not anyone on a regular. There was an old cat I had seen a couple of times at the grocery store who kept suspiciously showing up when I would be there. Marilyn was living off campus with another soror, while completing her Spelman transfer hours. Her and her boyfriend were going through their usual ups and downs, but she would never tell me any details when it came to him.

The current job I had wasn't sustaining my current lifestyle. I kept thinking that I would get a better paying job at some point. I got an apartment from the remaining monies from my Pell grant and student loans. One day, this old cat finally got my attention and expressed he wanted to get to know me a little better. I figured this could be the break I needed to get on track with my money. This could be the perfect situation. Since he was older, I figured there was no chance of anything happening seriously. This could work to my advantage.

He had a nice car, dressed well, and smelled amazing. After I introduced myself to him, he made it clear that he was married, which was fine with me. This meant he wouldn't have much time to spend with me. Dang, this situation was getting better and better by the minute. A married man was perfect because I wasn't a threat to his marriage. I could care less about having any lasting feelings about him.

I thought about the many conversations I'd had with my mom about not wasting my time with a man if he couldn't do anything for me, especially a married one. She told me as long as I had that stuff between my legs, I should never be broke. I didn't understand what she was saying at the time. I knew she wasn't trying to pimp me out – that was clear. It all made sense at that moment what she had been telling me all those years. There was a demand, and she had the supply.

She had three kids to care for, and she wasn't passing up any opportunities. I never understood that as a child why she felt the need to mess around with married men all the time. This led me to think that all married men cheated on their wives because she made it seem like the demand was high. After Hank, all the men she dated were kind and good to me and my sister. I know she had some battles with a few, but after that monster Hank, my sister and I were never again subjected to any sexual or mental abuse by anyone. I'd already made up in my mind that I wouldn't go for it.

I decided to mess around with this married man. I hadn't gotten a good job yet and time was running out. We started hanging out at my place. It became apparent real soon that I had to come up with an excuse as to why I couldn't have intercourse with him. He was buying weed for me, spending money on me and making it clear he wanted to get sexual. I had to find a way to tell him I couldn't go all the way.

My brilliant plan was to tell him I was a virgin, and I wasn't ready for all that. I thought this was a clever excuse, but even my naivete didn't realize that was an aphrodisiac for him. He was getting turned on even more by the thought that he would be my first. I needed him to take it slow with me and be patient because I had no intentions of sleeping with him. I thought if I let him perform oral, I could then act like an inexperienced sexual and curious girl.

Throughout my short life at this point, I had learned the importance of having an exit plan. I had been in many situations where I needed to know how I would get out of a tight situation. This relationship could only last for a short period of time because I would eventually have to put out. He loved the way I danced. I had used my dancing talent many times as a weapon. I used it for more than winning dancing contests with my mom. I would perform an exotic dance routine mixed with my stylish skills for him.

This was very selfish and manipulative behavior on my part, but I didn't care. It was a demand, and I provided the supply in this situation. I am aware that the proper terminology is supply and demand, but in my case and in my mom's case, it was demand and supply. These married men felt they needed, or should I say demanded, to have an on-call sex partner whenever it was convenient for them. I was only providing the supply for that demand.

Things were about to change because I needed something more than just a little spending change and weed. I needed to get my rent and car note paid. I got emotional and shared with him about my financial problems one night during one of his visits. He quickly volunteered to take care of it all for me. It was an instant sense of relief throughout my body. I was very grateful for his response, but still not grateful enough to sleep with him.

After living a promiscuous lifestyle during my freshman year at Bishop College, this was not to be the case at UCA. I had not slept with anyone but May, especially not a man. I thought maybe the time had come and I should finally sleep with him to show him my gratitude for taking care of my rent and car note. I don't know why I felt I needed to do that because that was not the plan from the get-go. Yet I felt an obligation to reward him. I had decided that I would do it at the end of the week, but we didn't make it that far.

It was a lazy afternoon, and I was laying on the couch just relaxing from a nice joint I had just smoked. There was a knock at the door. I thought it was him so I went to the door with the intent of letting him know this was the day I had finally made up my mind to sleep with him. I was ready to jump his bones. When I opened the door, it was the sheriff's office with an eviction notice. I had one hour to get out, to get everything I could, or everything would be put on the street. I was high as hell thinking to myself, 'What the hell?' He told me he had paid the rent – had even shown me the receipt.

See the old man had pulled the same shit I had pulled on my aunt. I guess he had an exit plan as well. I was shocked and didn't know what the hell to do. I thought I would grab my stuff and head to my car and figure this out. When I looked down at my designated parking space my car was gone. Damn! This was getting worse. Not only had he not paid the rent, he had only made a partial payment towards the car note, hence the repossession. I was homeless and had no way of getting to class. Marilyn knew about my relationship with this man and she was good to go with it because if he was taking care of me, she was fine.

But here I was again in another hot mess, all because I relied on someone else to take care of my needs. Just like with May, I had turned over my independence and willingness to do for myself to someone because they had shown a slight capability of taking care of my material needs. I had once again settled for convenience. I had adapted an attitude of laziness for convenience. I may have made some strides, but I was still weak, and the only person I knew to call was her.

I made my way to a pay phone to call Marilyn. When she answered, she was surprised it was me and said she almost didn't answer. Immediately, in my voice, she detected that something was wrong. I told her what happened. She knew of my plan and before I could finish talking, she said, "I will get someone over there to get you." She explained she was with her boyfriend and she couldn't come herself. I told her that was fine and that I would call my uncle. She screamed, "No! I'll get someone over there. We don't need the family to know this right now. You stay there. I promise you. Someone will be coming soon. Stay by this phone and I will call you back."

About twenty minutes passed and I was getting nervous, thinking maybe she couldn't get anyone to come get me. Then the pay phone rang. It was her telling me someone was on their way and would give me a ride to the trailer. The trailer was the place she was sharing with her boyfriend and another soror. Then she said, "I told soror what happened, but she is cool. So you be cool, relax and be yourself. I will see you later." She then closed the conversation with, "It will be okay."

~MJ's Journey~

When I received the call that Wilma was evicted, I panicked. I knew telling her family was not an option, primarily because of all that had transpired with May. Taking this on as a personal project would create additional havoc to what was already present in my relationship with my boyfriend. Putting aside helping her was not an option because I knew what she would do if the tables were turned. It was clear that the dynamics of my living arrangements would be drastically change. I had so many things going on. This was the last thing I needed to take on. Between struggling with the UCA/Spelman fight of merging my hours, trying to stay on top of things in class, attempting to keep up with my boyfriend, not to mention trying to make sense of the myriad of feelings towards Wilma, I was spiraling. Helping Wilma out of this bind had to be done, but I was overwhelmed.

The soror showed up liked she said. She was Marilyn's childhood best friend. When this soror was pledging, I wasn't the nicest person to her. She pledged during the "May" timeframe and I was out of control back then. She had a car full of people when she ran up to my apartment. She looked at me and said, "Soror, the people in the car don't know anything about what's going on. We will just act like you are storing some stuff at our place okay." Marilyn had relayed to her that I was to be treated with care and respect, like their friendship depended on it.

Soror showed up with grace and dignity and came into my apartment to let me know she knew what was up. I walked to the car with my clothes in a bag and a few items in my hand. Everyone in the car was high, so I don't think anyone paid much attention to the fact that I was homeless. I was to sleep on the couch for the night, I thought, and head over to my uncle's place in the morning – or figure something else out. Marilyn had decided I could stay as long as I needed to. She knew I needed time.

~MJ's Journey~

*When Wilma moved in, I took personal responsibility for her well-being. This undertaking widened an already very present wedge in my relationship with my boyfriend. He repeatedly discouraged the growth of my relationship with Wilma. I made it clear with him that she was family and my soror and **not** dealing with her was not an option.*

The major apprehension about this change, the moving in, was the risk of someone that cared about me actually witnessing my truth. It wasn't that there would be four adults squeezed into an 1100 square feet trailer; It was the reality of what happened within those walls.

When she walked in that night with him, I was on the couch. She asked how I was doing, and if I needed anything. I told her I was good. As they headed to the back toward the bedroom, I suddenly realized I had never been around them as a couple in an intimate situation. I knew I had changed and had worked hard at controlling my emotions, but what if he was mean to her. How would I react? I had no reason to believe he was mean except the fact he was an overall contentious fella.

Since there had been an old rumor about Marilyn's boyfriend

slapping her in the high school cafeteria, I was somewhat concerned about what I would witness while living there. My Aunt Heavenly had asked about it one day when we were playing cards. Of course, Marilyn denied it, made it seem like it was no big deal and that she had control of the situation. She claimed the information my aunt had was wrong – that it was not an altercation or a slap and not quite like the rumor that had been spread around.

I couldn't hide the constant smile on my face when she was in my presence. How was I going to react in front of their relationship? If I couldn't disguise my own admiration for her, how could I stay there. At that point in my life, nothing was more important than having Marilyn as my friend, so I would keep my emotions intact at all costs.

There we were – Marilyn, her man, a soror and me all living under one roof. Soror spent some nights at other places, so it was basically just me living with Marilyn and her man. I finally got a good job, but it was still a few weeks before any money would come through. Without fail, every time Marilyn would leave, she would discreetly ask if I had money. She never wanted me to be anywhere and need something and not have my own money to get it. In a way, Marilyn had assumed the role of my protector, but I wasn't going to let her continue that way. I needed to know for myself, and also show her that it was my job to protect others because that's what I'd done all my life. I had defended my brother when he was bullied. I taught my sister how to defend herself and I waited up late nights to meet my mom on those dark stairs to protect her.

Chapter 12 ~ A Life Taken, A Life Given

I heard the phone ringing inside the trailer, then it stopped. After what seemed like seconds, I heard a heart wrenching scream come from inside. I went running into the trailer, and there she was sitting on the floor crying uncontrollably.

* * *

I was working at my new job all the time and not seeing Marilyn much even though we lived together. She had started becoming more and more awkward toward me and we didn't talk as much. Sometimes when I would approach her, she'd become standoffish. I decided in my mind this had nothing to do with me, but one night I approached her to catch up with her. She told me she would be going home for a while. I was extremely disappointed, but I thought to myself this is something she needs to do. Then things took a strange turn. She asked me not to call her when she was at home. I'm thinking well damn maybe this does have something to do with me and I asked why. She asked me to just respect her wishes. Okay, I agreed. She was tripping hard for some reason. If she was fine without talking to me for long periods of time that was fine with me. I caught an attitude and sarcastically responded, "Fine! That's cool with me. Whatever!" She left for about a week. I missed her, but I honored her wishes and did not contact her.

~MJ's Journey~

Telling Wilma that I needed to go home for a few days to handle some personal affairs made her livid. I was on a wild emotional rollercoaster and had no room for her hurt feelings. Unbeknownst to her, I had been dealing with some health issues along with mixed emotions about us while attempting to make sense of an abusive relationship.

For the last four months I had been treated for excessive bleeding, tumors and cysts on my ovaries by the quack I had trusted for over a year. Then one day, I received a call from the specialist that I had recently visited who had quite a contradicting verdict. **I was pregnant**! My very first and original fear was if I would have a healthy baby? Secondly, what the hell was mama gonna say, and strangely enough, there was the concern of how to tell Wilma.

The two-and-a-half-hour drive home felt like forever. The ride was full of tears, apprehension and fear. Mama and my brother Alexander, aka Alex, were home. Since they didn't know I was coming, they were shocked to see me and immediately asked if everything was okay. I asked them both to sit down so we could talk. When I told them the news, they hurriedly and simultaneously said that I would get an abortion. I was adamant against doing that. I was six months pregnant. Since over the past few months I had consumed a cocktail of medications with many procedures to treat the cysts and tumors, at this point I needed the primary concern to be focused on the health of the baby and myself.

Instead, my mom and brother pulled out the yellow

pages. Alex made phone calls to inquire about an abortion. He found a clinic in Dallas, Texas that would perform an abortion up to a six-month pregnancy. I was hysterical, shocked and couldn't believe that he was serious. I couldn't get out of there quick enough. I kept thinking about what a disappointment I had become to those that expected more from me.

When I returned to Conway, I was elated to see Wilma, but nervous about the talk I needed to have. When I told Wilma that I was pregnant and that I took the trip home to tell my mom, she was everything I needed – compassionate, understanding and a friend. My head space had changed. No more drinking or smoking. I instantly switched into mommy mode and so did Wilma.

I had not told my boyfriend the news. He never showed much interest when I was battling with health challenges so I doubted that he would have much interest in this life-changing milestone. I did know that he was definitely not going to be okay with the thought of Wilma being the Godmother, but that was not up for discussion. I was excited to ask her, but knew I had to at least tell my boyfriend that I was pregnant. I wasn't sure when I would tell him either piece of the news because he was seldom around. He was always blatant with his affairs and when questioned, more than an argument always ensued. As expected, telling him the news of me being six months pregnant was uneventful. He was more concerned with my relationship with Wilma and his relationships with everyone else.

This news came at the most challenging time because I was scheduled to return to Spelman, if it was determined that my computer science classes would not transfer. I would be forced to take them at Clark College. Luckily, Spelman accepted the hours of the computer classes that they didn't offer, but there was still much coordination needed in order for me to pull this off.

I felt so relieved that maybe Marilyn's time away wasn't about me. My reaction was one of excitement for her if she was happy. I asked why she didn't tell me and why she left for a week. She said she had to go home to talk to her mother, which she knew would be hard and needed space and time. She was visibly upset and scared because she knew she wasn't supposed to get pregnant in college. She wasn't sure about anything at this time. With tears running down my face, I said, "Okay, great! Now we have a baby to take care of. You will be a great mom and I got your back." She was shaking as I put my arms around her.

Her conversation with her mom had not gone like she wanted it to go. She needed me at this moment to be a friend, an emotional and stable friend so I hugged her. We sat there for hours with my arms wrapped around her. We cried and we laughed. I made up in my mind that I was going to be there for her and this little person. She told me she was scared because she didn't know if she was ready, but she had to be ready because this was her miracle baby.

I didn't push her on what she meant at the time. I just wanted to be present for her in that moment. She didn't need words from me. She needed a friend to amen her sentiments and offer an assurance that I was going to be that for her with every fiber of my being.

After she shared that information with me, I felt like I had to work harder at everything from that day on – my grades, my work. I needed her to know she was going to be fine. I started saving money, working more hours preparing for her new arrival. I knew she had a man and that was his job. Anything I did would be extra for her new baby. She had saved my life literally, and I wasn't going to let her be fearful of not being able to take care of her child.

I knew Marilyn had many friends she was close to and had grown up with. I was the new friend on the block, the one that was borderline crazy to everyone else. She started to bring me around some of those friends and one night, while playing cards at another sorors' house, someone asked who would be the baby's Godmother. Like everyone in the room, I expected her to name one of her childhood friends. She looked up from the cards in her hand and said, "Wilma Jean." I was shocked as everyone else in the room, but I didn't act like it. I just took it in stride. My insides were jumping up and down with excitement.

Trusting me to take care of her baby meant she believed in me. When we got into the car, I asked her why me and she said, "Because you love me. I know because you love me you will love my baby. And there is no one who will work as hard as you to make sure the baby will be okay if anything ever happened to me." Before she could complete her sentence, I said, "Happen to you?" She responded with a chuckle, "Yes silly. That's what Godmothers are for – to take care of the kid if something happens to the parent."

It was a nice spring Saturday afternoon in the month of April, and we were hanging around the trailer cleaning and listening to music. I was outside smoking because ever since Marilyn had announced her pregnancy there was no smoking in the trailer. I heard the phone ringing inside the trailer, then it stopped. After what seemed like seconds, I heard a heart wrenching scream come from inside. I went running into the trailer, and there she was sitting on the floor crying uncontrollably. "What's wrong?" I screamed. She just continued to cry. I picked up the phone and it was her older brother. He asked if she was okay and I said, "What's going on?" I could hear someone in the background saying, "Alexander, Alexander. Oh, Alexander." Her oldest brother was on the phone and asked if her boyfriend was there and I responded no, but that he'd be right back.

He told me to stay with her until her boyfriend returned home because their brother Alexander had just passed away. It was Alexander that told Marilyn he thought I might like her in a special way. Alexander was her ace, her best friend at the time. She loved him. It was him she told her secrets to.

He had struggled with addiction problems and had a massive heart attack. She was heartbroken. I picked her up from the floor and sat her on the couch trying to reassure her that everything would be okay. I was asking her to please pray. I couldn't find the words to comfort her. Then I said the only prayer I knew, the Lord's Prayer. We needed Jesus' presence in that moment. I was so nervous I would mess up the words, mismatch verses, but she knew I was trying.

She looked up at me with those tantalizing eyes and that intoxicating grin and said, "Thank you." Her boyfriend walked in the door, saw her crying and started freaking out. I guess he thought it was something to do with the baby. I immediately told him that the baby was fine, but that her brother Alexander was dead. She then jumped into his arms and I walked back out the door.

~MJ's Journey~

In the midst of all these life altering events, the phone call telling me of my brother's untimely death was worse than anything that had transpired. Although he had battled a drug addiction for years, he was doing well and was finally in a good place. If he could have distanced himself from those 'friends' that did not have his best interest at heart, his quality of life would have been much better. These were the same 'friends' that sneaked drugs in the hospital and rehabilitation facility for him. Because of his sickness, open heart surgery was performed in Detroit, Michigan years prior to his death. The surgery performed involved the removal of three heart valves. During this time, there was no such thing as an artificial valve replacement, which meant he was the only man known to live with one heart valve. Alexander had a massive heart attack and succumbed to his death in my mama's arms. This shook my core because he and I understood every secret shared. We were very close and had a special bond. Wilma understood this and did not disappoint in being there for me.

We were scheduled to head to Helena on Friday for Alexander's funeral. Marilyn left earlier in the week. Although the baby wasn't due until the end of the month, the phone rang at the trailer and it was her telling me the baby had been born. The baby was ten days early and an emergency surgery was performed. I asked her, "Why did you go and do that? I was supposed to be there. Are you okay? Did you say girl?"

Yes, it was a beautiful baby girl. When I asked what she had named her, I anxiously waited for her to tell me one of the names she had written down prior to the baby's birth. She said, "Alexis, I named her after Alexander." I was speechless and overcome with emotions. I tried to hide that from her because I never wanted her to see that part of me. That was the most absolute sweetest act of love and quite a way to show respect for her brother.

I calmly said, that is a beautiful name. She asked if I could come the next day instead of waiting until Friday since the baby had been born and everyone was busy with the funeral arrangements. They didn't want her to go to the funeral, but she insisted that she was going. Then in the most infectious voice she said, "I need you to be here tomorrow." I said yes without hesitation even though I had no idea if I could get there the next day or not. When I got off the phone, I cried because her miracle baby was here.

I had a piece of a car, but it was in no condition to make the two-hour trip to our hometown. I was dating a football player at the time and we had been going steady for a while. I asked him if he could take me to Helena but Soror Catherine, Marilyn's best friend from childhood, finally got back in touch with me. I had put the word out around campus that I needed to talk to her. I asked her if she could take me to Helena the next day. She said she could, but didn't have gas and would need to wait until Friday. I told her I had the money and asked if we could hit the road as soon as possible. Although my football friend could not take me, he made sure I had the gas money I needed.

We got there the next day and it was like I was seeing her for the first time. She was glowing and beautiful as ever. And then there was Alexis. The first time I picked her up I felt an instant connection. She was gorgeous. My heart started beating fast. She was everything. I felt like I was supposed to be holding her in my arms. There she was my little Alexis, my Godchild, my baby girl.

~MJ's Journey~

At the time, not going to my brother's funeral was a tough pill to swallow. I realized later, not being released from the hospital for the funeral was the best thing that could happen. The stress and grief extended an early invitation to my first born. I was released from the hospital the day of Alexander's services. Of course, I stayed put for a few weeks. It was really weird being at home, but even more so, grieving while being a first-time mom, which proved to be a blessing in disguise.

Chapter 13 ~ Secret Lovers

"Let me hold you tight, if only for one night. Let me keep you near to ease away your fear. It would be so nice – if only for one night. I won't tell a soul. No one has to know."

* * *

We made it through that period of grief and heartache and I returned to UCA. It would be a few weeks before Marilyn returned. The plans were for her to return for the End of the World Show at school, which would also be around her birthday. I was planning to throw her a birthday party as a celebration for the birth of the baby as well.

When Marilyn went home, I was basically homeless during that period. I stayed at the trailer when I was able to, but I had other places I lived as well. It didn't feel right staying there without Marilyn present because she was the reason I was there. I stayed at a couple of weekly motels. I tried to hide this from everyone. I was determined that no one would ever see me vulnerable and unable to take care of myself. When one of my sorors gave me a ride home, I asked her to drop me off across the street from the motel. She sat in her car without me noticing and watched me cross the street to the motel. She came to my room and I was surprised to see her standing there when I opened the door. She asked if there was anything she could do and if I needed a place to stay. She lived in the dorm, but she was willing to let me sleep on her floor if I needed to get away from this place. This motel was near a truck stop with a bunch of old men hanging around all the time. I told her I was in between places and assured her that I could protect myself if I needed to. I asked her to keep this to herself until I got my own place.

Marilyn's boyfriend was hardly at the trailer through the week and he'd go home on the weekend to be with Marilyn. He stayed for a short period of time back home right after the birth of the baby. His sister started staying at the trailer for a while as well.

I had spoken with Marilyn every night while she was back home. Our conversations had become the cornerstone of our friendship. Even if we had spent an entire day together, we'd still call each other on the phone all the time. I was getting blow by blow details of Alexis' activities. I had seen her a couple of times during weekend trips.

When Marilyn returned to Conway, we were getting ready for the party. A keg run was needed and she wanted to ride with me. As we were riding, she talked about how happy she was to be back and especially glad to be back here with me. I thought the same and I let her know that. As she moved closer to me, she said, "I really missed you." I said, "Girl I have seen you and we've talked every day." She said, "I know, but being with you just feels good." She was acting different. Over the course of time, our friendship had teeter tottered on a cliff, but this moment felt like we were on the very edge of that cliff. I asked her how she was doing overall. Instead of answering, she wanted me to listen to a song and tell her what I thought about the words.

We had to wait to get back to the trailer before I could hear the song since this was before Google and YouTube. We had to get back to a record player. When we got back to the trailer, I asked her what song she wanted me to hear. She put on this album and these words came across.

"Let me hold you tight, if only for one night. Let me keep you near to ease away your fear. It would be so nice – if only for one night. I won't tell a soul. No one has to know." The voice singing was the silky, sexy, soulful voice of Luther Vandross. It was a song on his new album. The words sounded as if she had written them herself. My knees got weak when the song said, "I won't tell a soul." That verse sounded like she was standing next to me whispering them softly into my ear.

I knew what was happening, but I wanted to make sure she also knew. It was a very moving song with beautiful words. I really liked it, but I had to remain composed. She told me she loved those words and they made her think of me. I wanted her to know, if we go 'there'; she needed to be fully aware of what we were doing. I didn't have the strength to resist her because I was in love with her, and all I wanted to do was to touch every part of her body.

I knew that her and her boyfriend had some real issues with him screwing other women. I needed for her to address those feelings and make sure she wasn't doing something because of him and his actions. He had gotten involved with a girl on campus. A couple of sorors and I paid the girl a visit, to remind her that he had a woman and that woman had just given birth to his child.

I responded to her comments about the words of the songs and said, "Words without actions are just words." At that moment, her boyfriend's sister walked into the trailer. She was ready to get the party started. We would have to return to this conversation later – or maybe never again. At this point, it was time to party.

There were plenty of parties going on around campus that night, but that didn't stop our party from jumping. We had people showing up at the trailer that we had no idea who they were. The liquor started getting low, which was fine because we needed people to leave and there would be no more liquor runs. Everyone started to leave, but I did not want to be there with her alone. I kept thinking that she may be drunk and I didn't want that conversation to start again. I left to go to another party. I didn't drink or dance at this party. As a matter of fact, I was a bit of a dud because I kept thinking about her and that song.

When I decided to go back to the trailer, I was hoping that everyone had gone home. She was the only one there when I walked in. I immediately sat on the couch, which was still my bed when I would stay the night. As soon as I sat down, she asked me if I was ready to talk. I looked at her and said, in a very stern voice, "Okay let's talk. What are you asking me to do with that song?"

She looked at me and asked me to tell her if she was being selfish. I needed to know if this feeling she was having was just curiosity or if it was genuine. How could she ask me that knowing that I was in love with her or maybe she didn't know how I really felt about her. She was on my mind all the time. Although I dated one guy on a regular and we were an item, he was sweet and had all the things I liked in a man – masculine, dark and well-built, but we had no emotional connection. He gave me the cover I needed, so he was really just a place holder.

Marilyn returning to school was all I thought about and often wondered if I should tell her how I felt about her before we did something that we could not take back. I asked her if she knew how I felt about her and she interrupted me before I could say, "I think I love you." She said, "That's why I trust you with everything about our friendship." She told me that she would never do anything to hurt me. There was no one I trusted more and I believed her with all my heart. I had to do everything to make her think about that.

I started to tell her she was being selfish and very unfair. Before I could finish, she grabbed my waist and pulled me toward her and kissed me passionately. It was like we had been kissing for years. The kiss flowed with ease as we embraced each other with an instant fury of flames. The heat from my body was bursting through my pores. As easy and relaxed as it felt, I knew what I was about to do would forever affect everything about us and our families.

I kept thinking about what my Aunt Heavenly said. "You all can't do that." Was this all worth crossing a line that would greatly affect more than just us? Holding her in my arms just felt right and she seemed so at ease with me. I knew at that moment I was signing on to be a part of her life by any means possible. I would do whatever she wanted me to. I had to brace myself for what was about to happen. Was I mentally ready for this? Did I truly know what this meant? I was about to permanently entrench myself with the label of black sheep of the family. Not only was I about to sleep with my uncle's best friend's woman, but a friend that was also considered family.

I was about to sleep with another woman, something I knew was not acceptable in my family or society. None of that mattered at that time. The only thing that mattered was making her happy. I had resolved that I would do whatever made her happy at all cost. Marilyn had become to me the most important person in my life at this point. She had helped pull me up and taught me how to walk around with my head up. I wasn't shameful anymore. I felt alive and was actually enjoying life.

She had prayed and cried with me, listened to every one of my farfetched ideas and at this point, she needed me. She was confused and a little lost, but I loved her. I knew deep down inside I would never do anything to hurt or embarrass her. I would behave myself and keep my emotions intact. No one would ever know how much I loved her. I would go to my grave without telling a soul if that gave her happiness, contentment, and security.

She had the softest skin I had ever touched. The passion we felt for each other led us into his sister's bedroom. We connected with every touch. I had taken a mental picture of each part of her and remembered every single thing about that night – from those little bitty ankles, to that long beautiful black hair and her sweet fragrant scent.

The intensity of the moment prevented us from hearing the front door open, but I did hear footsteps. I put my hand over her mouth, pointed to the door and then jumped into the closet. His sister started calling her name, and Marilyn responded in a loud voice, "What? I'm in here." I'm in the closet thinking, 'Oh no, what the hell are we going to do?'

Suddenly, I hear Marilyn say, "I'm sorry I laid down in your bed and fell asleep." Marilyn then asked her if she was ready to go to bed. I'm in the closet freaking out because I'm thinking, 'Ready to go to bed? Did she forget I was still in the closet?' The sister asked where I was and Marilyn immediately said without hesitation, "Oh Man! Did you forget that she asked you to come get her at 1 am?" The sister then remembered when we left together to head to the other party, I had asked her to come back for me, since she was planning to return to the trailer before me.

When she was leaving to pick me up, she asked Marilyn if she wanted to ride with her. Marilyn was always good and quick on her feet under pressure. When I eased out the closet, we were silent for a minute, wanting to make sure the sister was gone. We looked at each other and burst out laughing. I asked if she was okay. She smiled and said that she was great. When she asked if I was good; I smiled back without words.

The next morning, while laying asleep on the couch, I was awakened by a push to my shoulder. It was Marilyn; she mouthed under her breath with a big grin on her face, "You still good?" I smiled back and asked, "How about you?" She assured me she was fine with a wink of the eye. Not soon after that, everyone started waking up and moving about the trailer. How were we going to act around other people? We pretended like nothing had happened last night. We all talked about the party. She shared her plans of going to Spelman to meet with her advisor to finalize the transferred hours. That was not a conversation I was excited about hearing, but I knew she would return to Arkansas... eventually.

I went about my business with an occasional smile during the day. It was the most awkward situation. I was hoping no one would ask me why I was smiling because I wanted to shout to the world how wonderful last night was. I believed in my heart that might be the only time I would ever sleep with her. I was hoping that didn't affect our relationship and we would always remain friends, no matter what.

In the meantime, I headed to work. I had an excellent job with a road construction company and was making good money. The company was owned by an older black man named Mr. Walter. He was from a small city in Arkansas that wasn't far from the university. He had several contracts with the State of Arkansas, employed several college students and also gave second chances to people who wanted employment. Mr. Walter was a good man. It was fascinating to watch him run his business. The white men that he negotiated with would talk to him as though he was not intelligent. I was intrigued watching him make power moving decisions and ponder over employee issues.

Everyone that worked for him had his back. When he needed things formally written for any type of submittal, we would all step up to help him. We never wanted any of those white guys to treat him like he didn't have his business affairs intact, or treat him like he was not a big deal because he was a big freaking deal to us. He always had money and was a very generous man. Seeing him own and run his business made me think this was the norm for black people.

I didn't realize, until later in life, just how much of an inspiration he was to me. During this time in the southern state of Arkansas, he was showing me what black excellence looked like. We all looked up to him. I did have to make it clear to him in the beginning that I would not sleep with him. Once we got that established, he became a father figure to me. I could call him for anything. He helped many times when I was homeless and living from motel to motel.

When I saw Marilyn later that night after work, she looked

perfect. She seemed to be in a good place with no remorse, and she didn't hate me. But I needed to talk to her about last night to make sure. She asked if I wanted to get some food, so I jumped on the offer immediately.

As soon as we closed the doors of the car, she looked at me with the biggest grin on her face. When we pulled completely away from the trailer, she said, "WOW! I have been freaking out all day." I asked her why. She repeated the word "why" in a perplexed voice. Looking at me like I was crazy she said, "Only thing I've wanted all day was to see you." Then she kissed me with those soft lips, but I really wanted to talk first. "Wait, wait. Are we good?" I asked. She looked at me and said, "All I know is that last night was better than I had imagined."

We always looked for opportunities to spend time together and at times we were a bit reckless in our behavior. Marilyn had said many times that she cared about me. I knew she loved me as a friend, but something began to feel different.

We spent the entire day together talking about whatever crossed our minds. We could talk about anything and it never seemed like we got tired of each other. On this particular day, Marilyn looked at me and said, "You know what? I really like you a lot." Before I knew it, I said in a sarcastic voice, "LIKE ME?" and I laughed.

She grabbed my face and looked directly into my eyes as though she was looking through my soul. I was not accustomed to seeing such a serious face, especially in our moments of intimacy. She said, "I love you and I think I have a problem because I'm falling in love with you." I gently kissed her and told her that I had loved her for a while and I asked her what she wanted me to do. Her response was a few simple words, "Just love me for now." Those words were all I needed to hear. She told me just to love her for now, and I could do that.

Our love for each other grew over the next two years and we were inseparable. I had become a permanent side piece sworn to silence and getting time with her whenever I could. I had also embraced my new role of Godmother with Alexis and we had become extremely close. I was focused and content. Rumors were circulating throughout the campus, but when people thought about Marilyn, the notion of her being gay would go away quickly because she had a boyfriend, a baby and didn't fit the role of a stereotypical lesbian. She had even been questioned by her boyfriend about me. He'd inquired about our closeness. She was constantly reminded to be careful of me. I was still that crazy chick that ran around with the hippie white girl. It was becoming increasingly hard for us to be around each other in the presence of others. Despite all the rumors and assumptions, we maintained our friendship and still spent most of our time together. I would have the occasional boyfriend around for a front, but it didn't matter because all of my attention was devoted to Marilyn and Alexis.

It was getting close to graduation and we had been in our new house for a couple of months now. Everything was moving smoothly until one day I had to be on campus early in the morning. My car would not start, and I needed to make this managerial finance class. It was a course I needed to receive a grade of at least a "C" average in order to move on, as I had taken it before, ending with a "D" average.

I needed a ride and one of my buddies lived too far to come get me in order for me to make it to class on time. This meant I had to go ask Marilyn to take me to class or use her car. Even though I knew they slept in the same bed, I had never gone into their bedroom. We had strange living arrangements. I would spend quite a bit of time away from the house, so I wouldn't be around them as a couple. However, I would make myself available anytime if she needed me for Alexis. Whenever she needed me for Alexis I would do it without hesitation. I would be there in an instant. Alexis was the most important thing in the world to me. We would coordinate my schedule to spend time with her.

So, there I stood at the door of their room in a real dilemma.

The last thing I wanted to do was knock on their bedroom door, but I had to get to class. I gently knocked and put my ear to the door to wait for a response. Time was getting close. I wanted to wake her but not him. I gently knocked again with my ear up against the door. I thought I heard someone say come in, so I opened the door to enter. She popped her head off the pillow. This was the first time I saw them in an intimate position. I felt a jolt to my emotional existence, instantly questioning what we were doing.

I was very apologetic, but not phased because I had to get to class. I told them how sorry I was, but I needed a car or a ride to class. She looked at me and then looked at him, then back at me. "I'm out of here as soon as I get someone's keys," I said. She told me her keys were on the table in the living room or in her purse. When I got to class the shock had finally worn off, and I was starting to feel jealous. I couldn't concentrate the entire time in class.

After class, I returned her damn car immediately. For the last two years I had never gotten angry or upset with Marilyn except for the occasional last minute reschedule of our hook up. But for the first time I had seen her as his girlfriend in full force. I knew they had problems. I guess I had resolved in my mind that she was not with him. In my small way of thinking I had replaced him. I had to get myself together because I was getting furious. I wanted to make her feel like

I felt. I decided I would go hook up with one of the few girls on campus who had shot me some vibes.

When I entered the house, she was there with Alexis. Alexis greeted me with a contagious big smile. I returned her keys and thanked her. "No problem," she responded. "I got your car started." I turned to ask what else she did that day. She looked at me and angrily replied, "I know you are not at this time going to do this." I said, "You are right. Not at this time."

I grabbed my keys and headed to Little Rock for the night. She asked where I was going. All I could say was to the club in the city. When I said the club, she knew what I meant. There was a nice gay club in Little Rock that we had gone to a couple of times. We really enjoyed going to the club because we could be free with each other, dance and just get into each other with no worries. She enjoyed my dancing. She looked at me and said, "Okay fine. I'll see you when you get back."

I went to the club with a buddy, met a few girls, danced and went back home. I thought of her all night and didn't want to lead anyone on with my actions because I didn't want to hurt her. I loved Marilyn. All I wanted to do was protect her and never hurt her. I got back to the house and as usual he wasn't there. She was up watching TV and Alexis was sleep.

I walked in with zeal determined to show her I was okay and

wasn't upset anymore. I asked her how she was doing, but she didn't respond immediately. Then she eventually said, "I'm good. Did you have fun?" I told her the club was slow, not much going on. She said I was lying. "You danced and had a good time and I know you did because that's what you do." I told her I needed to apologize for earlier and she quickly let me know there was no need to apologize.

She said, "We both know what we're doing and it's just me and you that know everything. Don't ever lie to me again. Promise me that because it's enough lying going around, and we can't lie to each other. We're going to keep it real with each other." I knew exactly what she meant. Then she said, "I know you danced and had fun, but I also know you didn't do anything. I just need to know that we will always be straight with each other." Looking her straight in the eyes I promised and said, "I will always be straight up with you and never lie." Then I kissed her on her neck and walked toward my room. I always felt a sense of security and comfort whenever I spoke with her about things. Her words had a way of calming me like nothing I had felt in my life.

Marilyn had become the most encouraging person and my biggest cheerleader. She was way beyond confident that I would finish school. She believed that I would graduate from UCA more than I believed it. I had endured too much to not make it. I had been homeless, occasionally living in motels and many times, I was jobless. I had embarrassed myself, my family and my sorority. Before I walked across that stage there would be one more humiliating incident that would lead to the most challenging event to test my newfound emotional stability.

I left for class one Friday morning, then headed straight to work on the road crew to work about four hours. When I got back to the house, all of our things were on the sidewalk. We had been evicted. Marilyn had gone home for the weekend, so I called to find out what was going on? I had been paying most of the rent at the new house.

In a fearful voice I asked her what was going on, and if she knew they had put everything on the street. Then she said, "I was hoping to get mama to give me the money." I angrily said, "What do you mean *give* you the money?" She started to cry. I realized she was really upset. I didn't know her boyfriend hadn't been paying his part and her mom had been covering it. Marilyn's mom had been adamant about her returning home or to at least bring Alexis back, and decided she wasn't going to help anymore.

I didn't want to make her feel any worse. I asked about my portion and she said she had it. I assured her everything would be okay and not to cry. I asked her if she would be coming back, to which she said probably not. "Keep the money," I told her. "I will be okay for the next couple of months and I love you. Everything will be okay." I just wanted to assure her of that.

Chapter 14 ~ New Horizons

So, I decided to come straight with the job and tell them. That I need to complete one more course to receive my diploma. This was a very awkward conversation considering I had misled them.

* * *

I knew I had not done well in this Managerial Finance class, but I thought I would make it. Hell, I was only three hours short for my degree. I had spoken with my instructor and he knew this. He was aware of the heartache and some of my struggles while at UCA. As I sat in my advisor's office, all I could think was please don't make me come back and take this class. I was going to march across that stage because I had earned and deserved it.

He began to tell me, "You will fall short of the 120 credits needed to receive your degree for the May graduation but you can march and complete the hours over the summer." Here it was 1987 and I was about to get a Marketing Degree from a university in Arkansas. Yes, me – a little old troubled queer-curious girl from the projects of Chicago.

I had left Bishop College because I was convinced a degree from a small black Methodist college in Dallas would not bring the kind of job I wanted. Yet, I could not help but think that my conversation with the professor about my personal plight to get to this point would have been received differently if I had remained at Bishop.

I had managed to get this far and I had to complete the race. There was no room to doubt my decision now. Never expect someone to feel your waves when riding the surf of life. From that moment on, I realized I had to make it my way and keep my struggles to success to myself and share only with the ones who cared.

I was so happy and hoped everyone in the family would be as well, but that was not the case. My grandmother was excited and certain I'd go back in the summer to finish. My sister was also ecstatic but to everyone else in the family it was just a simple ceremony. Some thought I shouldn't participate in the ceremony, until I finished the three hours needed. It didn't matter because I was excited and most of all ready to leave Conway. I had become tired and complacent.

I walked across that stage three credit hours short of the 120 credit hours needed. When my grandmother, sister, myself, and of course Marilyn left that morning headed to Conway for the graduation, it didn't matter to us that I had to come back in the summer. It really didn't matter that it wasn't a "real graduation" as some people in the family had considered. I was going to this ceremony because I had made it through, what at times, was a living nightmare, an utter embarrassment for myself and my family, I needed to show people that I completed this disastrous race.

~MJ's Journey~

After all the emotional ups and downs, the financial setbacks, trying to sort valid feelings versus invalid, figuring out my life as a new mom, the one constant that paid off was the back and forth from Atlanta to Arkansas. I was determined to piece meal my college credits and make happen what so many said couldn't. Being a college freshman while also a senior in high school was non-traditional and definitely a struggle, but it was worth it. Nothing was more challenging than doing that and staying committed to all the summer sessions, while pulling strings and finagling three different universities and colleges to merge my education and send to me what I had earned. My life in Atlanta was full of heartaches and disappointment. I was so thankful to leave there and know that I could still accomplish what I set out to do without having to remain. Permanently returning to Arkansas was not on my bucket list, but making sense of it was now on my personal agenda.

I needed to get away from Conway for a while, so I decided I would go back for the second half of the summer courses. I went to Helena to live with my grandmother and came across a job offer for a trainee with an investment company in Memphis. They were looking for new employees for entry level jobs. I applied for the job claiming I had received my degree. In my mind it would be just a few more months before I had the real paper. I was still within the time frame to say I was waiting on the actual diploma. I had an unofficial transcript, but it was still proof of my attendance at the university. Hell, I'd just completed five years of education focusing on marketing and business – surely, I could sell myself to this company. And I did.

I was accepted and saw this as an opportunity to get started in the business world. It would be a forty to forty-five-minute drive from my home with a training period of three months. The downside was no pay. My return to summer school required money. How would I be able to do that? I had financed my entire education, and now that I was a five-year student, I'd received the max amount allowed.

On top of that there was an out-of-pocket fee to be paid in order to receive my broker's license. I had concocted in my mind that if I got the job then I could show my worth and value. Hopefully, any conversation about my degree would be non-existent. But there was still no answer to how I would pay for the broker's license. I had no actual paying job and no money saved.

If I was going to make it big, I needed this job. I would be learning about the stock market, how to invest and analyze potential investment opportunities. I was willing to take the chance and go for it. The training would prepare me to pass a series of exams in order to sell, buy or advise on the purchase of stocks.

I asked my grandmother to loan me the money and assured her I would pay it back. She was told by another family member not to lend me the money because I didn't have a job, so how was I going to pay her back. My grandmother had another idea. She figured she could help and teach me a lesson at the same time. She had a life insurance policy on my mother, along with other policies on other family members. She approached me about cashing in the policy she had for my mom. She also took this opportunity to share with me the importance of preparing for the unthinkable.

She wanted me to promise to take a policy out on my mom for much more. She made it clear to me that is what people did to make sure their loved ones were taken care of at the end. It would be my responsibility to make sure my mom was taken care of. I promised to take a policy out for my mama when I finished my training, so she cashed out one of the policies.

Meanwhile, Marilyn was going through some trying times of her own. Our hook up times began to decrease and her boyfriend had decided to move before school ended in May. He left and went out west to be with his mother. They were having some serious issues – things she never shared with me and I never asked. I figured she would tell me what she wanted me to know. I didn't have the money to return for the second quarter of the summer nor did I have the time. So, I decided to come straight with the company and tell them that I still needed to complete one more course to receive my diploma. I thought it would be a very awkward conversation considering I had misled them. Thankfully, it went better than I expected. I was allowed to continue with my training with the understanding that it was to be completed before being brought on permanently.

Living with my grandmother was a blessing for me at the time because I couldn't afford to pay rent. I had no income and the only way I was able to get to work was by borrowing money and using credit cards. I had received an American Express charge card in the mail not too long after graduation. I used it to purchase gas and take care of myself, but wasn't paying any money to my grandmother to live at her house. I didn't think it was a problem since I didn't ask her for money and bought a few groceries.

~MJ's Journey~

Being an adult and living with my mom, brought about many difficult times and being a new first time mom made it even harder. There were times I just knew I would pull my hair out, one strand at a time. He was no longer my 'boyfriend' but now my baby's daddy. He had decided that going out west to his mom's was what he needed to do. At the time, I thought that was best. I began to convince my heart that the right thing to do for Alexis was encourage her dad to marry me...marry us. I needed to give this a chance and see if what everybody thought was the right thing for me, was really right... for me.

~Our Two Cents~

We were entering our adult lives. We had touched levels of our emotions that we didn't know was possible and still fighting feelings of uncertainty. If we were to move forward to become the adults we were destined to be, we needed to embrace our true selves. We knew this wouldn't be an easy task and we didn't know if we were up for the battle. Some of us are late to the party of maturity, but when reached we need to engage in the celebration of one's growth.

Section Three

Chapter 15 ~The Choice

As I sat there in the car shaking and crying, this old gentleman ran out from his house and asked if I was okay. ... I immediately yelled, "No..." He said, "Okay. I will go get you some water, but I need you to move real soon girl."

* * *

One beautiful afternoon in 1987, Marilyn called and said she needed to talk to me. She sounded serious on the phone and it felt like a cloud was starting to form around my beautiful day. When she got to the house, she wanted to sit on the porch to talk. The first words out of her mouth were, "I owe it to Alexis to do what is right. I can't keep going back and forth with him." I knew what she was about to say. A lump grew in my throat, but it was no time for me to fall to pieces or even show any resentment. I could see she was struggling to complete her thoughts. She finally gathered her composure and said they were getting married.

I took a deep breath, even though it felt like I wasn't breathing. I didn't cry and I didn't get emotional because what was I thinking anyway. There was no way we could do this forever. Then she said, "I want you to still be a part of my life and I definitely want you in Alexis' life." There it was – the one statement I needed to hear to be able to move on from this news.

I could now totally concentrate on my new job and being there for Alexis. I wasn't over Marilyn and I still loved her, but I was going to cooperate and go along to get along. She said she was getting married – not that she was in love, but because it felt like the right thing to do. After that news, I couldn't stop thinking about her all day. The thought of her getting married and picturing her in a wedding dress brought a smile to my face, but moments later came a tear, but I remained calm.

I started struggling with the training program after passing my first series test. The drive to Memphis was getting old and my car was not in good condition. I had a few mechanical issues, so the fear of it stopping any moment was always there. One day while driving through Mississippi, the car started shaking, and I thought maybe it was about to stop. I was so deep in thought that I was not paying attention. A dog appeared to be closer than it actually was. I swerved to miss it and lost control. I ended up on the shoulder headed straight for a cotton field. When the car hit the gravel, it started to spin. I could feel my heart beating through my clothes. I took my foot off the gas pedal and squeezed the steering wheel as hard as I could, trying to regain control of the vehicle. Finally, I reached a grassy area that allowed me to slow down.

As I sat in the car shaking and crying, this old man ran out from his house and asked if I was alright and did I need him to call someone. I immediately yelled, "No. Just please give me a few minutes and I will be fine." He said, "Okay. I will go get you some water, but I need you to move real soon girl."

I sat there and started to slowly get my composure together. At this point in my life, I had never told anyone about all the things that pained me. I was good at keeping things to myself and that had now multiplied by ten, since the May incident. I never wanted that relationship to be front and center of all my shortcomings or failures, especially after such humiliation. I felt if I showed any signs of weakness or vulnerability, people would think I was weak mentally. Everyone knew Marilyn had just told me she was getting married. I didn't want anyone to think this accident was a cry from me or a sign of me falling apart again. So, I didn't want anyone to come and assist me.

The car would start, but I had a flat tire. When the gentleman returned, I let him know I just needed to change it. He said, "Well you are on your own on that because I am on my way to pick up my wife. You can wait on me to return if you want to." Then he looked at me and said in an emphatic voice, "If I were you, I would get it changed quickly. It's getting late and you don't want to be in these parts when it gets dark." I could have taken that a lot of ways. I was on a highway in Mississippi by myself on someone else's property. I took it as a warning to hurry up and get my black ass out of there. I told him I knew how to change it and I wouldn't take long.

June '87, time was approaching and it was starting to look like this wedding might really happen. She then dropped the bombshell that she wanted me to be in the wedding. What the hell was she talking about? I'm still thinking in my mind there's not going to be a wedding. Now, she is asking me to be in the ceremony. My immediate response to her request was "Are you serious?" "Yes," she replied. "You should be there. You are Alexis' godmother, and you are my best friend." I'm thinking 'Okay this is really happening', and I still cared about her so much.

I respected her so deeply I could not let her hear the sound of disappointment in my voice. I felt that Marilyn was going to be in my life forever and she would eventually come around. I was reminded of the words from *Midnight Train to Georgia*, "I would rather live in her world than live in mine without her." I was convinced Marilyn was in love with me. Maybe she was in love with both of us, but I felt we connected on another level. Plus, she had never told me she loved him, and I held onto that with every hope of her being mine one day.

The job in Memphis was falling apart, and I needed more work. I decided to take on an evening part-time position as a security guard. I also started to see an old friend from college who was back home as well. We spent quite a bit of time together. I enjoyed talking with Cassie and felt comfortable around her, but I would spend every minute thinking about Marilyn. I hadn't mentioned that I was seeing Cassie again until one morning while leaving her house. My uncle was outside in his truck at the house next door picking up a co-worker when he saw me walking out. I knew he would bring it up in front of Marilyn. As far as she knew I was only dating a friend of her boyfriend.

He looked as if he knew I was feeling guilty about something. When we made eye contact that morning, I think he knew I was in love with Marilyn. He had seen me around guys and heard my conversations about them, yet I think he knew my reaction that morning had nothing to do with a man. I needed to get to Marilyn first, but it was early in the morning and I had to be at work in Memphis. By the time I would get back he would have already had the opportunity to tell her.

Nothing had been going right with work. I wasn't performing up to standard. I was failing my exams, and all of a sudden it felt like I wasn't worth waiting for to complete my degree. I felt like they were about to ask me to leave. So that morning when I went in, I asked to speak with the supervisor. I told him I had appreciated the opportunity. I knew it was a field that could yield an extremely high income and would be a game changer, but I didn't think it was for me. I had no idea how I would even build clientele because everyone I knew didn't have money. I explained how this was a big mistake on my part. He simply said that he understood. He asked if I was sure because he thought I was underestimating my talent. Talent? What talent did I have? I had left Bishop College for UCA and made a complete ass of myself. Plus, I had fallen in love with a family friend's woman.

This was just another failed endeavor for the girl from the projects of Chicago with a big imagination. I continued to listen and asked what he meant by my talent. He said, "You have a strong and unbelievable spirit about you and that makes people feel comfortable being around you. That will go a long way in this business. We cannot teach that. Naomi, people like you." I expressed my appreciation, but I was broke and needed to make money.

Before I walked out the door he said, "Go back and finish your degree. It will be helpful, but only if you make it work for you." I knew the conversation was hard for him because he was the one, I talked to the most about my degree. I apologized and expressed to him I didn't mean to lie or be misleading, as my intentions were always to go back and finish. He said, "Like I told you Naomi, you have an uncanny way of making people like you and trust you. Please use that wisely."

When I got to my car, I thought what the heck had I just done. I thought maybe I didn't give this a chance, that I should have hung in there longer. I cried for about five minutes, but I had to get home to get to Marilyn before my uncle saw her. I had to make one stop first. I had come across some information about the military. I thought back to my days in Chicago when I first thought about joining the Navy. I was hoping to get more information about the reserves to gain some extra income, but I didn't want to move far away from Marilyn and Alexis.

I went straight to my aunt's house to see if my uncle had made it home. She was surprised to see me. "Why was I over so early when I should've been at work? Why was I looking for my uncle?" I just wanted her to stop asking me questions. I'm the one who had questions. When my uncle walked in the door, he asked me how things were coming along with the wedding. I told him as far as I knew all was well. Now I didn't care if my uncle thought I was a whore, but I didn't want him to tell Marilyn he saw me leaving Cassie's house that morning.

After being there a few hours, it was becoming a little weird hanging around. My uncle went outside to smoke a cigarette on the porch, so I took this opportunity to talk to him. I went outside, and he looked at me and asked if I was okay. I said, "Yes. And oh, about this morning…" He said, "Oh yeah. You don't have to worry about me talking to Heavenly or your grandmother. You're a grown woman; you can do whatever you want to." I looked at him and I took a big sigh and before I started to talk, he handed me a cigarette and said, "You don't have to worry about me telling anyone about your business." I took a drag of the cigarette and felt a sense of relief. I could feel him looking at me, but I didn't know what he thought at the moment.

We were close to the day that Marilyn would be getting married and I was to be in the wedding. I had not felt well for a few days. One day while going through the final details with Marilyn I felt faint and rushed to the restroom. I threw up all over the bathroom floor at my grandmother's house. Marilyn looked at me and immediately said, "It will be fine. We will get through this." There was no doubt that we would, but I let her know that I hadn't been feeling well lately. She then touched my forehead, and I didn't feel warm. She asked what else could be bothering me. I told her I had been tired, nauseous, and feeling sick to my stomach. She asked me about my period. My period? What did that have to do with anything? She asked when I'd last had my period. I told her I didn't keep track of my period like that so I didn't know. She said, "Wilma! You might be pregnant." There was no way I could be pregnant because I hadn't had unprotected sex. No, I couldn't be pregnant because I just couldn't be. What in the hell was I going to do with a kid?

Chapter 16 ~ Yep, It's Happening

We would spend every minute together since I would be gone for two months. Obviously, this started to put a strain on her new marriage.

* * *

~MJ's Journey~

Going through many motions with plenty emotions, it all seemed like an outer body experience. A choice between doing what appeared to be the right thing versus what my heart was directing me to do. I kept telling myself that this is what God, my fiancé, my mom, my baby girl, the community and society wanted. At the time, in my mind, my desires were not an option. A wedding was being planned that was completely coordinated by his mom and mine.

During this entire time, I was so worried about Wilma's physical and emotional well-being. The news of her pregnancy brought about a large amount of relief – maybe not for her, but definitely for me. I saw it as an opportunity to prove to EVERYBODY, especially MYSELF, that our relationship could be seen as a pure friendship and not treated as it really was. Even still I had refused to believe she could possibly be pregnant. I had convinced myself it was nerves and stress. It had been a lot for her to digest. It always felt like I was going through so much, but when the entire situation was assessed, she was the one going through the most. I was making choices she was being forced to accept.

A rainbow represents a sign of hope and promise of better times to come. It was appropriate for June 6, 1987 to be identified as a day for a "Rainbow of Love". All the maids in the wedding were dressed in pastels and there stood, third in line, my best friend and the one that I loved. Little did I know that my real rainbow was filled with primary colors and not the palette of pastels.

On *that* day I stood there with other childhood friends watching the one person in the world I loved more than anything else say "I Do" to someone else. As the tears ran down my face, I'm thinking how could this be happening. Here she is getting married, not to mention the fact that I was pregnant by a man who loved another woman. I wanted neither of these things to be true.

I had decided to join the military prior to the wedding. I was due to leave in eight weeks, but now I was pregnant. I hadn't shared with anyone but my sister and Marilyn. I had to decide what I was going to do and soon. I had made up my mind I was not about to have a kid in the current situation I was in, but that was selfish of me when there was also a father involved. There had been a few incidents at my grandmother's house that made it clear his live-in girlfriend knew about our relationship. We had come outside to flat tires and busted windows a couple of times. I told him I thought I wasn't ready to be a mom and I didn't want to live in Helena. We both decided that I would have an abortion. It was an emotional conversation. I felt in my heart of hearts my baby would have been a boy. It would have been my great honor to name him Chris after the very first man that loved me.

After my abortion, my body needed time to heal before leaving for boot camp. Even though Marilyn and I had not engaged in any sexual activities since her marriage, our bond together was growing stronger and stronger. We would spend every minute together since I would be gone for two months. Obviously, this started to put a strain on her new marriage. We had tried not to spend as much time together, but that did not stop the amount of time we spent talking on the phone. I was looking forward to going to boot camp because it would give some time for things to cool off.

Chapter 17 ~ Boot Camp

The instructor jumped in and helped me to the side. He was breathing hard and yelled, "Are you okay recruit?" "Sir, yes sir," I responded. He then said, "What the hell is wrong with you? Why did you jump off the platform if you could not swim?"

* * *

The day had come and I was off for eight weeks of boot camp. I would be back in a couple of months as a member of the United States Military Reserve and *finally* making some money. Hopefully this meant that I would be able to go back to school and complete my degree. My Aunt Heavenly and a close friend of hers drove me to Memphis to spend the night, then I headed to Philadelphia, Pennsylvania. I had said my goodbyes to Marilyn and Alexis the night before. Everything was going to be fine. I would be gone for eight weeks. Everything would slow down and at the very least, the conversations about me and Marilyn would stop.

We arrived at the base late into the morning with only two hours of sleep. We had to get physicals, take shots, give blood and urine, have uniforms issued, and a whole lot more. I was poked and prodded everywhere. I noticed that all the girls in my company were being told they would be going on to the next phase, which was the swimming and physical testing. I was told by a medic that I would need to stay at the medical dispensary so the doctor could talk with me. I sat there waiting and waiting. Everything bad started running through my mind. Was I sick? Had they discovered something I didn't know I had? This was the most intense and comprehensive medical exam I had ever had.

Finally, the doctor entered the room and said, "You're pregnant, young lady." I said, "That's not possible." He says, "I have the test right here in front of me. Why are you so sure you're not pregnant?" My brain could not comprehend what the doctor was saying at the moment. Was I being punished for having an abortion? All I could say was, "Sir, I just had an abortion about five weeks ago; I can't be pregnant." He looked at me and said, "Well that's the problem. After an abortion, you can still test positive up to six weeks after the procedure."

I could not believe what I was hearing him say to me. Was I still pregnant? He started talking about HCG (human chorionic gonadotropin) hormone levels. He said sometimes it could take up to two months for those levels to drop. I started to come out of the daze I was in. He stated it was unfortunate they couldn't continue with the processing even with a false positive result. It needed to be negative to continue. The process consisted of me returning to my recruiter and receiving instructions for what to do after that.

There I was in Cape May in the medical unit waiting on my paperwork to process me to go back home. I talked to my recruiter and he informed me that I could come back in a few months but to make sure I didn't test positive as pregnant again. I didn't want to tell anyone about this, especially Marilyn – not right now. I called my aunt and told her I would be back in two days. Then it dawned on me I had not told her about the abortion. This was something that would need to be addressed when I returned.

I didn't tell Marilyn much about what happened over the phone. I just wanted to get back home and lay low for a while. When I returned to Memphis, my uncle picked me up. He was an ex-marine, so he had a lot of questions on the ride back to the house about my quick return. He thought I had lied about something on my application, or didn't pass the medical exam. I told him there was a problem with my physical, but I could return in two months. I don't think he knew what to say. He asked if it was drugs and I told him no. I think he knew I didn't want to talk about it so he handed me a cigarette and simply said, "You look like you need this really bad."

I went home with the intent of keeping myself out of sight. The phone rang, and it was her. She asked what happened and I told her. Then she asked if I wanted to see Alexis. Of course I wanted to see her. She said she would bring her by, but wouldn't stay. She sounded a little distant and cold, but I was okay with that because I was getting to see Alexis. For the next two months I saw a lot of Alexis but truly little of Marilyn.

~MJ's Journey~

Wilma's unexpected return brought mixed emotions of which I was determined to manage – both hers and mine. I desperately tried to interact with her in a way that was not misleading. I didn't want to send mixed messages or give any false hope to anything. How was I to do that when all of my emotions and feelings were nothing but jumbled, muddled and confused? I spent quite a bit of time trying to get my husband to understand that, in spite of his thoughts, I had every intent of making sure that Alexis had a positive and strong relationship with her Godmother. I was looking forward to the time that Wilma would be away. It would allow the time needed to reflect on my marriage and prove to him that Wilma was not the problem in our relationship.

I returned to Cape May and this time I was ready; I had made sure of that. The first night was just like the previous time, so I was not shocked with the tone and language of our CC (Company Commander). I made it through the medical exam with flying colors. I was set and ready to go to the next phase, which was the physical and swimming test. I hadn't been swimming much, but I knew how. I could keep afloat, plus we would be swimming every day. That meant that I would get to practice and perfect my skills. I was in excellent shape. I had always been very athletic, so I never feared any physical activities.

When I saw the pool, it was large and deep. I started to get nervous because I had never been in a pool so big. 'Okay,' I'm thinking to myself, 'If I don't make it the first time, I will have time to get better.' As we were walking up the steps to a six-foot platform, I turned around to one of my fellow recruits and shared that I didn't think I could swim well enough to jump off. She looked at me and was blown away with what I'd just told her. She kept saying over and over, "What do you mean? What do you mean? Can you swim, Recruit Scales?" I told her I could swim, but I was afraid of heights, and didn't think I could do this.

We were not supposed to be talking and now the instructor was pissed and yelled, "Come on recruit. Get to the platform and jump." My fellow recruit told me to tell him so I wouldn't get hurt. There was no way I was going back home. I had to suck it up and just do it. Hell, I had lived on the ninth floor of the projects, so why was I afraid of heights. This was different because there were no boundaries to protect me.

I got to the edge, closed my eyes, jumped, and hit the water headed straight for the bottom – at least that's how it felt. I came up above water and started to struggle a little before doggy paddling. I had damn near knocked myself out. I was now in survival mode. The instructor jumped in and helped me to the side. He was breathing hard and yelled, "Are you okay recruit?" "Sir, yes sir," I responded. He then said, "What the hell is wrong with you? Why did you jump off the platform if you could not swim?" I said, "Sir, because you ordered me to jump, sir." He looked at me and said, "Get your butt to the locker room." The other female recruits came into the locker room saying, "You're crazy as hell. Why did you do that?" I said, "Because I don't want to be reverted back to the next company." They went on about how I could have drowned and I said, "Hell, I'm here with the best swimmers and rescuers in the world. I was not going to drown."

My CC informed me I was the worst swimmer he had ever come across and should be reverted and damn near put in remedial swimming. Then he proceeded to say, "I ought to send your ass back home." I only said, "Sir, yes sir." The swimming instructor was a young black man and he had assured my CC that I would be fine after one week in swimming training. I wasn't sent home, but I did have to get up one hour earlier than the rest of my company in order to train. I became a leader by default because I was older than any of the women in my company. I was good at all the physical activities and a lot of girls feared our fourth week physical training (PT) test. I helped them with proper techniques for doing pushups and pull ups.

Finally, the day had come. All the ladies had completed their PT test, including the swim portion. They were all free to go to the locker room. I was the last person to swim. I think my instructor thought I needed to swim without the other women staring at me. Boy, was he off. All the women returned and positioned themselves at different intervals along the length of the pool to cheer me on. While learning to swim freestyle my shoulder popped out of socket, so I jumped in and swam the best way I could. I had to swim using the side stroke instead of the traditional freestyle stroke.

Every moment of tiredness was met with a scream of, "Come on! You can do it Scales." The ladies in my company, one by one, pushed and encouraged me to finish. When my hand hit the wall in the final stroke, I was exhausted. My heart was racing, but thankfully, my shoulder had held up. Now, I had to get myself out of the pool, but they couldn't help. They all stood there until I gathered enough strength. We were not supposed to show any kind of emotions. Completing a swim test was not supposed to be this big of a deal, but it was to us and definitely helped solidify our bond as a unit. The instructor turned his head and walked away. We were one-for-all and all-for-one at that moment. All the girls yelled my name with high fives, hugs and chants exchanged.

Everyone looked forward to mail call when we would receive letters from loved ones. Everyone always knew who would and would not receive mail, so it could be difficult to watch a fellow recruit not receive anything. I experienced that the first couple of mail calls. Then finally my name was called, and I had received five letters on one day. I was so excited at the thought of everyone writing me from back home. I had one letter from my sister, but there were four letters from *her*. Some of the fellow recruits asked who this person was that had been writing me every day. She would only use her initial and sign it with our sorority secret signature. We could not take a chance of someone knowing that these letters were coming from a woman. If there had been any thought that I might be gay or bi-sexual that would have become a problem for the military. Even though the letters were mainly about Alexis, she would let me know just how much she missed me and the word love was used a lot. As we got closer to the April graduation, however, some of her letters started to take on a tone of nostalgia from a friendship standpoint. I wasn't sure how to take that.

We had our final exams and PT test. Because I had been in remedial swimming, I had to pass both. My fellow company recruits only had their final in PT to complete. I took the swim test first because the PT would be a breeze. The breeze was actually the swimming. I jumped in, swam, and finished my test with flying colors. I was extremely fatigued from the swimming, plus I had started my monthly cycle. I did my sit-ups and my run. The only thing left was my push-up test. I could do push-ups in my sleep, but as I began, my arms started shaking and I couldn't put the pressure on my shoulder to push myself up.

I'd finally made it to the end. After seven weeks of bonding with my company, excellent classroom grades, all the physical activities, and marching together; the excitement of finding out where everyone was going for their first duty station awaited us. I was a leader in this company and had called the cadence when we marched. The ladies trusted and looked up to me with all of my wisdom, wrapped up in a 22-year-old girl from Arkansas. We were all excited about our pass for the weekend to get away from the base and get ready for graduation. Unfortunately, I didn't pass my push-up portion, not once, but twice. I was devastated as the instructor had to revert me back a class to the Romeo company.

I was ordered to head to Romeo's barracks. When I got to the Sierra barracks to get my sea bag my fellow recruits could tell immediately something was wrong. When I started retrieving my items, they wanted to know what was going on. As I shared that I didn't pass my PT, the looks on their faces were of confusion and disbelief. Some thought I was lying because they just couldn't believe that I didn't pass the PT portion. That was one of the most difficult days of my life having to walk out of that barracks and say goodbye to the young ladies whom I had grown to respect and care about. I felt like I had disappointed them in a way. How could I be a leader if I couldn't perform the required tasks?

Chapter 18 ~ Times Have Changed

She reached for my hand and I pushed her away and got out of the car. ... I told her we were done, and I needed for her to leave because I could not promise that I could keep it together. ... she drove alongside me for a second until I screamed, "Leave!"

* * *

~MJ's Journey~

When I received the call that Wilma wanted me to pick her up from the airport in Memphis, I was elated and my emotions became mush. I was so excited that I would get to see her, but knew I had to remain subtle when making moves that involved her. Things at home had been awful. I was miserable, but I did not want to share any of those things with her. I wanted to spend time hearing about her experiences. My primary objective with Wilma was to convince her that we could be friends, the best of friends if we did this thing right. Although I was determined to set the precedent that we would keep our status as best friends and sorority sisters, it was impossible to tell my heart the same. When we saw her at the airport, Alexis was super excited. She picked her up and gave her a huge hug. I squeezed her just tight enough to feel those boot camp biceps and triceps and definitely long enough to smell that jheri curl juice...my aphrodisiac.

It was May of 1988, and I had finally graduated. I was excited to see Marilyn, but nervous. I didn't know what would become of this visit. I arrived in Memphis with a pocket full of money. When I got off the plane there she was with Alexis. Alexis took off running toward me. I had my sea bag around one shoulder and a teddy bear for Alexis in the other hand. When I saw them both, I was overcome with emotions. I had not shown many emotions since my first night of boot camp when my CC told me to stop crying because crying wasn't allowed inside those walls. I did not cry, but my heart smiled and then my face followed.

I picked up Alexis and gave her the biggest kiss all over her face. She gave me the biggest and tightest hug as she called me "her auntie". There she was standing there beautiful as ever, but she was even more beautiful this day. She walked over to me and asked if she could get a hug as well. We smiled at each other and as soon as I put my arms around her, I felt safe and at ease like I had always felt. She had a very tight hold and gently kissed me on my jaw and said, "Welcome home."

Even though I felt at home in her arms I also felt something else as well, like a sense of calmness about her like she had made up her mind about something. As we headed to the car she asked if I wanted to hang out for a while and stay overnight in Memphis. When I agreed I also wondered how she could do that. She had a husband to get home to. She assured me not to worry, it would be okay. When we got to the car, she pulled some flowers from the trunk, handed them to me and said, "Congratulations on your graduation. I wish I could have been there."

~MJ's Journey~

The stay in Memphis was filled with laughter, shopping, hugs, dining and re-securing a bond that I thought I had broken. We'd spent the day playing with Alexis and the time had come to put her to sleep. Wilma and I drank and talked all night. One could feel the sexual tension between us. Even though we'd connected that night emotionally like never before, the ride home was quiet and filled with unspoken apprehension. We were headed to reality and I knew I would have a million questions thrown at me. I felt confident in my answers being the truth. Yes, I had a great time with Wilma, but in my mind, it was all innocent. I just had to convince my heart and him otherwise.

I had shared with Marilyn that I had given some thought to going active duty, but I didn't want to be too far away from Alexis. After I reported for my thirty days of active duty as a reservist, I was warming up to the idea of going active duty full-time. I really needed the money, and I could complete college. I would give more thought to it if I couldn't find a good job after my thirty days.

My time with Marilyn was now being shared with other family members around, so we didn't get much alone time. I could feel the tension when we were all together in the room. Then one day she wanted to talk, but she wanted to meet somewhere private to talk. We met at one of our many secret hook up locations. If she thought I was about to be with her after the cold receptions she'd given in the presence of others, she was about to be shamed. I needed some explanations from her about her coldness.

~MJ's Journey~

While Wilma was gone, my husband had asked that I sever ties with her and focus 100% on our marriage. I relied on the distance between her and me to help figure this out. This was one of the toughest decisions I had made in life. Not only did I love her, but I knew it was important for her relationship with Alexis to exist. It was important for her, Alexis and me.

I needed to talk to Wilma and I wanted us to meet in a safe place to share our emotions, and one that would bring the comfort needed for the talk. It was the discussion of the dreaded decision. It needed to be a place where our most vulnerable, raw and intimate moments had occurred. It was foolish of me to think that any setting would soften the words.

When we met, I immediately noticed her eyes were red from crying. She was visibly upset about something. I had no idea what I was going to do if she was about to tell me that he had hurt her. I immediately asked what was wrong. Her mouth started to tremble, and I thought to myself, 'I don't want to hear what she has to say.' She said I don't know how to say this, so I want you to listen to this song.

Her request for me to listen to a song was different than her previous requests. My eyes started to water up as a sense of sadness came over me. Then I closed my eyes as the lyrics started, "If I should stay, I would only get in your way." It was a magical voice. I had heard this angelic voice before because I loved her music. I had a serious girl crush on her, but I had never paid much attention to this song by Whitney Houston. And she was singing, "I will always love you. I wish you nothing but love. I hope life treats you kind."

I opened my eyes and Marilyn was in a full cry, saying he asked her not to be friends with me anymore because he thought I was gay, and he couldn't trust me. She had to try and see if that was it. I'm thinking 'if that's it?' What did she mean? She had literally written the words to the song on a piece of paper and was reading the words to me. With tears running down my face I said, "Please don't do this. We are not doing anything. Please don't do this. What about Alexis? What am I supposed to do without you and her?" The thought of not seeing her was breaking my heart, but not seeing Alexis was a cross I wasn't prepared to carry.

She said she wouldn't hurt me by taking Alexis away, but how was I to see her if he didn't want us to be friends anymore. She reached for my hand and I pushed her away and got out of the car. She asked me to please get back in the car so she could finish talking. I told her we were done, and I needed for her to leave because I could not promise that I could keep it together. I walked away from the car as she drove alongside me for a second until I screamed, "Leave!"

~MJ's Journey~

After that exchange, I was an absolute wreck and no good for anybody – not my husband, my child or myself. That was one of the hardest things I had ever had to do in life. Having that conversation with Wilma was very difficult and not one I was in agreement with. I was going through all the appropriate motions and desperately trying to do all that was required and requested. My husband and I had a different definition of marriage. His definition of marriage was simply the legal union between a man and a subservient woman. Mine was the opposite of everything we were. I made a commitment to do all I could to make my marriage make sense.

She drove away and I collapsed against my car. I was crying so hard my body was hurting and I threw up everything in my stomach. I sat on the ground against the car wheel crying for what felt like a lifetime. I was devastated. I had kept my feelings and my love for her a secret, and we had this connection. Why was she doing this? This was like May all over again. I felt in my soul that everything about our relationship was meant to be. We were meant to cross each other's paths. She had to feel the same way as well. I couldn't be wrong about her. Nope, not her. Not this time.

She was my queen, my soulmate, my best friend. I wasn't wrong on this one. She just needed time and I thought I was giving her that time by not pressuring her for the past six months. I thought she knew I would be here waiting on her until forever. But why was she turning on me. She knew the deal. I couldn't hide the fact that I was a wreck and a mess.

The first person I saw when I returned to my grandmother's house was my sister. She could tell right away that something had happened to me, but she wasn't sure what. I put my head into her shoulder and told her what Marilyn had told me. Marilyn and I had never confirmed to anyone except to a few college friends that we were friends with benefits. We always felt that our secret relationship was safe with them because they were all living secret lives as well.

There was a circle of us at UCA that were living in two different worlds because it was the thing to do then. It was like we had our own secret club. But my sister knew that I was really good friends with Marilyn and that there was something special there. She felt my pain immediately. I wish I had come up with a better story to tell her that day because my moment of pain led to many years of a strained relationship between the two of them. She promised me she would make sure that I saw Alexis, even if it meant she had to go get her.

I told her I needed to get away with a fresh start and that I was going to go active duty. She wanted me to make sure, because this was the military. I felt that this was the time for me to go. I had entertained it in high school and the thought of servicing was something I needed to do, especially if I wanted to finish school. I immediately informed my superior. I would go to a base to await going to Class A school, and I had the luxury of choosing from a few locations nearby.

My sister kept her promise and would go get Alexis for me to see her. This did not stop the nights I would cry myself to sleep thinking about Marilyn. I kept wondering if she was missing me, if she thought about me, if ever I crossed her mind. The times I knew she was headed to my aunt's house I would leave. I couldn't see her so we never crossed paths. I had two weeks before I would leave for my new duty station.

Marilyn got word of me leaving for New Orleans, Louisiana. She asked my sister if I was going to see Alexis before I left. She and I hadn't spoken and I knew my sister didn't tell her. She would eventually call my grandmother's house. When I answered the phone, she asked if she could bring Alexis to see me before I left. I told her my sister was handling that and hung up.

The day came for my departure and my sister had set up my

visit with Alexis. Before we were scheduled to head to the bus station, she was supposed to pick up Alexis, but Marilyn asked to meet her at the corner store. When we pulled into the gas station there, I saw her car. I was not expecting to see her so I looked at my sister and asked why she was there. Her response to me was that Marilyn would not let her take Alexis. She wanted to see you as well. She explained to me all she wanted was for me to see Alexis and didn't know what else to do.

I walked over to the car and there was Alexis with this big ole smile on her face that always melted my heart. I picked her up and told her, "I love you and I will come home every other weekend to see you so we can visit with each other and play." I wanted never to break a promise to her.

Marilyn got out of the car and came around to the side I was on and said, "I have something for you. Just a few things for the bus ride." I could still see the color of love in her eyes. I was hurt, but I couldn't forget she had breathed life back into me. She had held my hand in my darkest moments, prayed for and with me and assured me that I was special and worth being loved. She had loved me for me and for who I was. I told her thank you. She hugged me and whispered in my ear, "I'm sorry."

When she stopped hugging me and pulled away, I could still

feel her presence and could smell that fragrance. I loved her from the very first moment . I was calm and had accepted the fact that I was losing her, but I was so thankful that she was my anchor when I was sinking. I could not hate her and could only love her. As she pulled away, all I could simply say was thank you and our hands slipped apart and she returned to her car.

She had given me framed pictures of Alexis and one of all of us together. She also gave me the words to that song by Whitney Houston handwritten by her with a few added lines at the end. She wrote, "I don't know if this is right, but this is what I must do. But know I love you very much and will always love you. You have touched me in ways I didn't know were possible."

~MJ's Journey~

The struggle of doing what others thought was the right thing to do was becoming evident that it was not going to happen if Wilma and I remained in the same city. Her leaving Helena again gave me a sense of relief because it had become impossible for my mind to control my heart. Our separation always allowed me to give my marriage 100%, but it didn't allow me to have love where there was none. This was the beginning of magnified lies, spoken and unspoken.

The day I gave Wilma a picture of the three of us, in my heart, I knew letting her go wasn't the right thing to do for us, but it was the thing for us to do right. That picture represented the future, my future, our future. I just had to figure out how and when.

Chapter 19 ~ NOLA: Who Dat Land

When I hit the bridge crossing over to the West Bank to head to the military base, it was 7:35 am. I made it to the base gates at 7:50 am, I ran to my quarters, grabbed my uniform, dressed quickly, and ran to the site for muster call with just a minute to spare.

* * *

New Orleans was the big city to me and my duty station was across the river on the West Bank. I was awaiting Class A school and all I had to do was follow instructions and stay out of trouble. Missing Marilyn turned into drinking and kicking it with the fellows. I was the only African-American female seaman at my unit. There were a few African-American petty officers, but it wasn't cool for them as second-class petty officers to hang with a seaman.

Most of the time I would hang with other seamen and airmen at the unit. This unit was special and we were a tight group. However, my black petty officer friends worried about me taking risks and putting myself in jeopardy before my Class A assignment. The only time we spent much time together was on the basketball court because there was no such thing as ranks on the court; we were all ballers. I was a tough sister that could ball and drink with the best of them. I balled with my brothers and drank with the white boys. One day one of the young brothers waited for me to finish a game. He just came straight out and said, "Listen sister! Lay low running with those drinking white boys so much. I don't want you to get caught up with the wildlife until you get your rate." He then gave me a dap and walked away.

I was the only sister in the unit until one day a sister petty officer showed up. She was wild looking and I was one hundred percent certain she was a lesbian, so there was no way I was getting near her. Her name was Sandra Bad. Yep, Bad was her last name. We had one thing in common; we were both from Chicago. I found out she had gone to Westinghouse High School, so we had a lot to talk about especially basketball. They had some big-name players that had come through Westinghouse, so she immediately got my attention. This sister could hold her liquor. I discovered this while hanging out with my black crew at the unit.

She was turning up on Crown Royal with the purple bag dangling and all. I drunk a little crown as well at times, but not like her. She was the coldest shit talker I had ever met. I had never seen anyone like her. She was extremely deep and a bit of a radical sister, but she was smart as hell and well read. One night she asked me who I was screwing at the unit. I looked at her like she was crazy. Then she said, "I know you're not tripping about me asking who you sleeping with." I told her no one. Then she said, "I like the white boys," and asked if I had ever been with a white guy. I told her no.

She had a foul mouth, but had a way with words. I had become used to it because most of the dudes in the military had foul mouths, but this was a woman.

We laughed and talked all night about the art of dating a white man versus a brother. She asked again if I was sleeping with anyone at the unit and I picked up my glass and told her no one. Then she wanted to know if someone at home had me messed up in the head and if so, they were not worth it. She stated in such a matter of fact way that there were too many out there. They come like ships – when one pass and you miss it, another will be coming by daylight. I thought that maybe it was time to move on from Marilyn, to open my heart to someone else. I had great appreciation for all my conversations with Sandra. We had connected as sisters. She had so many views on religion, race, eating, and natural medication. She was a different kind of sister, but she was one of the deepest sisters I'd ever met. I valued her friendship and often looked to her for advice.

One day my favorite Chief at the unit called me into the admin office. He wanted to know one thing from me and only one thing – had I ever bought drugs from the nearby projects. I immediately told him I had never done anything like that. He said I had to take a piss test and if it came back negative he'd have my back one hundred percent. I had no idea what chief was talking about, but I listened to everything he told me. He was the reason I wanted to be a Yeoman. He had shown and taught me everything I needed to know about how our job was to support the crew in any way they needed so they could perform the duties of our mission. Chief had unbelievable humility and a strength that was unflappable. He was one of the most respected chiefs at the unit. He could lead me anywhere.

One day I heard my name called from the mess hall. I was a bit surprised because I didn't receive a lot of phone calls at the time, but as soon as I picked up the phone, I recognized her voice. She was hysterical and crying so loud I couldn't recognize the words coming from her mouth. My heart started racing because I knew she was in tremendous pain. She kept saying, "They closed the curtain." She repeated this several times and finally I asked, "Who closed the curtain?" Finally, she said it was her mama and she'd had a heart attack. I heard what she said, but I didn't hear her say she was no longer with us. I asked where she was and she let me know they had her stable, but it was still very serious. I told her I would be there that weekend. I didn't know how I was going to get there but I knew I had to be there.

When I got off the phone, I immediately started trying to figure out how I was going to get home. Then there came a knock at my door and it was time to take the piss test. It was a female senior petty officer who had to watch me with the door open. I wasn't nervous about the test because I knew I had not been taking any drugs, but I knew I had put myself in some strange positions with a couple of my fellow shipmates. I had been in the truck a couple of times when a few shipmates went to the liquor store in that project area. I never really paid attention to anything else that was going on. To me it was just a couple of country white guys that I always hung out with and they loved drinking whiskey and I loved beer. I thought I made them feel safe or gave them some kind of covering when we went to the hood to get our liquor.

I took the bus home because my old car had broken down one too many times on my trips to and from Arkansas. While at home Chief called to let me know my orders had come down for me to go to Class A school, but they were on hold. This is what I had been waiting for – to officially start my Class A rating training in California. He also reminded me that this could all go away on Monday if the test was negative, but I would have to speak to the investigators again when I got back. Some issues had come up with some other testimonies.

I knew I had to be back on time as I could not take a chance of being late. In the meantime, I needed to buy another car. I had the money for a nice down payment and could afford the note. Unfortunately, I had bad credit due to the high bill I'd acquired with the American Express card received after graduation. At the time I didn't understand it was a charge card and not a credit card. All I knew was a card showed up and I had no spending limit.

Understanding money was one of the basic things of life I never learned about. I thought I could buy whatever I wanted since I had completed four years of college. I had been on my own since I was 18 years old. When I left Chicago and headed to Bishop College, I basically supported myself. Yes, occasionally, I would get some money from an aunt or uncle or cousin, but my everyday survival was ultimately my responsibility. I had worked just about every day since leaving Chicago. I worked in Dallas, Conway, Helena, Memphis and I was working now. I never wanted to see myself as being a victim or become too dependent on someone else, especially after things I experienced as a girl growing up. I knew I could not rely on anyone but myself. This was not because I thought no one would help with anything, but because I had become accustomed to taking care of myself. However, I realized now how so much debt and a bad payment history would make it very difficult, if not impossible to purchase a vehicle, but that didn't stop me from searching.

In the midst of spending time making sure that Marilyn was okay and checking on her mother's recovery, I was in the process of trying to find a car. I found the perfect one on Highway 20. It was a nice purple Buick Cutlass Supreme, but I needed a cosigner. I knew the perfect person to ask but time was running out. It was already Saturday and I needed to be headed back to New Orleans in order to make the 8:00 am muster call on Monday morning. I told the car dealer that I had someone for sure that would cosign. Well, at least I thought I had someone, but I was mistaken. When I asked my Aunt Jean to cosign, she may have been a little bit frustrated with a lot of things that were going on with our family. She didn't think I was responsible enough for her to be a cosigner.

I was devastated. I didn't know who else to ask. Since Marilyn had a good job at the time, she went to the dealership with me, but couldn't cosign because she didn't have strong credit either. My grandmother wanted to, but she had no income so they definitely weren't going to let her cosign. Time was winding down and I needed to figure out another way to get back. All the bus routes would be cutting it awfully close to muster time, which would also require a ride from the bus station.

The guy at the dealership was fantastic, plus he respected the fact that I was in the military. It was a small family-owned company. He said no matter what time of day or night to just call him when I had a cosigner. I had his full support, but I still didn't have a cosigner. My uncle was in a fraternity with a distant cousin of ours. This cousin had finished school and was working for the Arkansas State Police. He happened to be in town hanging out with my uncle so I figured I'd take a chance asking him to be a cosigner or else I'd be facing AWOL. I told him I would not let him down. I promised to pay for the car and not discredit him, but I needed it to get back to New Orleans. He looked at me and he said, "Okay Cousin. If you promise me you will pay on time then I'm good."

I Immediately called the guy at the dealership and told him I had a cosigner for the car. Because it was late, he didn't know if he could get the credit check completed, so he asked who the person was. I told him it was my cousin who worked for the state police and gave him his name. He recognized his name. Considering his line of employment and my military status that was good enough for him. He would run credit on Monday with the understanding that if it didn't work out, I would bring the car back to him.

There was a bit of time conflict because the guy was out of town. I hoped my cousin would be able to hang around to sign the necessary papers before he had to head back on Sunday. He told me he was not returning until later so he would be around. I started to get nervous as it got later and later. Finally, the guy from the dealership called and said he was having some family issues, but he promised he'd be back in time. As it neared 7:00 pm, the guy still hadn't arrived yet.

So now I needed to be looking for someone to drive me to New Orleans as this was cutting it close. He finally called and said he would leave around 10:00 pm. I thought there was no way my cousin could wait that long. I expressed my appreciation to my cousin and told him I'd try and find someone to drive me back. He knew I'd had no luck with that. He saw the desperation and fear in my eyes because this meant possible AWOL, and said, "Don't worry because I'm only about a couple hours away from where I'm going. I'll wait until he gets here."

Finally, the guy arrived around 11:00 pm. We met him at the office where my cousin showed his identification and signed the papers. I ran to him before he walked out of the door and hugged him and told him, "Thank you. I promise I will not let you down." He told me to be careful and drive safe back to New Orleans. I finished up and drove back to my grandmother's house to get my stuff. It was now 1:00 am and New Orleans was a six hour drive from my grandmother's house. There were no cell phones then. When I left that night headed down the back roads of Arkansas and Mississippi toward Louisiana, I had to be ready for whatever came at me – especially since no one had looked at the engine.

I reached the outskirts of Louisiana around 6:45 am approaching Metairie, but I worked on the other side of New Orleans in Gretna. Luckily, the downtown morning traffic hadn't quite started. When I hit the bridge crossing over to the West Bank to head to the military base it was 7:35 am. I made it to the base gates at 7:50 am, ran to my quarters, grabbed my uniform, dressed quickly, and made it to the site for muster call with just a minute to spare.

I could see my shipmates outside gathering. I found out later that many of them worried if I was going to make it in time. They knew this was a big day for me and were hoping and praying I did. Right after muster, call Chief wanted to talk to me. He told me my test came back negative. All he wanted me to say was that I had told them everything I knew, and didn't know anything else about the investigation.

I went in to talk to the investigators and they asked if I'd ever been to the Algiers projects. I told them exactly what Chief said to say. One of the investigators said, "You mentioned earlier in a statement that you went over there with a couple of shipmates. Are you saying that's not true?" I said I didn't remember. He said he remembered and asked if I wanted to write down what I said previously? I emphatically responded, "No!" I told him I would be glad to write down what I had just stated which was the same as Chief had told me. They thanked me and then dismissed me.

I immediately went to the Chief's office. I looked at him and he looked at me with his legs crossed in that familiar way he did all the time and told me to start working. I had many orders to process for PCS (permanent change of station) transfers including my own Class A order. Not sure yet if everything was okay, I just did as I was instructed and went to work. A lot of the guys that had been questioned were waiting on Class A school orders as well. I spent the whole day just nervous and praying that I would come across one of their files. The day finally came to an end, the investigators left, but none of us said anything to each other. I knew I hadn't done anything wrong, and all I had ever seen them do was drink a lot.

As Chief was preparing to leave, he asked me to walk with him to his car. As he stood there in the parking lot he literally got in my face and said, "When you first talked to the investigators it was their job to prove you had done something wrong. If you know you've done nothing then don't be stupid and give more than they asked for. You were stupid to run around with those guys, but the lesson here is you did nothing wrong. When you told me you didn't smoke any marijuana, I believed you because you are a believable person. Also, people will try to use your trusting nature and naïveté against you. Don't let people use your goodness to their advantage. I knew that you were very green and, as if all are as honest as you, the moment I met you. You damn near had a degree, but no one discussed with you about becoming an officer. Do your research, and never trust in the goodness of people without verifiable receipts. You can lead people with those qualities, be prepared at all times for anything."

He continued to share the difference between being smart and prepared, that I was born to lead (even if not in the service), and to never let anyone sell me short again. He then made me promise that I would keep my circle close and small and that my honesty and trustworthiness should be earned. I told Chief how I appreciated everything and would keep that promise.

Late 1989, I received my orders for Class A school in Petaluma California. It was time for me to leave New Orleans and head out west, but first I would return home. I visited with my grandmother and sister hoping I would see *her,* or maybe not. I didn't want to be a bother, but I could never go home and not see Alexis. She was the one thing that kept me motivated because I wanted her to have things from me as often as possible. I spent the next three days with her. I needed her to stay with me as long as possible because after this trip I wasn't sure how our future together would be. She would obviously be with her mom and dad, but I would be off to wherever the military led me. Alexis was only four years old and even though she couldn't understand what I was saying, I wanted her to know no amount of distance would keep me from her. If she ever needed me all she had to do was call and I'd do everything to be there for her. Every time she said "auntie" with so much conviction and love my heart would melt. I was afraid this time though because things were different.

Her mother and I were not connecting like we had in the past. I was going far away this time – more than just six hours away. When Marilyn came to get her before I left, I was filled with emotions. She had not been feeling well, which was expected because she was pregnant. She had called one day to tell me and my reaction was one of surprise, but I remained supportive.

I asked her how she was feeling that day and she responded not too well in a monotone voice. I was hoping she wasn't having any issues with the pregnancy. She immediately assured me it was not the baby, but a combination of other things. I could see sadness in her eyes, and I wanted to know if she needed anything. Even though our friendship was going in a different direction, her well-being was always a priority to me. She would never ask me for anything even though she had saved me many times in college, paid my way, kept me from looking bad.

I knew she needed something. I had received my advance for my trip, so when I kissed Alexis I reached into my pocket and pulled out whatever was in there. It didn't matter how much; she could have it. She didn't want to take it at first saying that I couldn't keep doing that so I told her it was for Alexis.

As I turned to walk away, she grabbed me by the shirt, pulled me back and gave me a hug. She whispered in my ear, "You deserve someone to love you, and I'm sorry if I hurt you. I never meant to do that. I thought I was doing what I was supposed to do to give my marriage a chance." Yes, I was hurt and sometimes angry at her, but I couldn't let her see that. I simply replied, "I knew what I was getting into. I would never hurt you like I did May, bringing havoc into your family. But don't you ever think I didn't want to fight for you." Tears ran down my face and I headed back into my grandmother's house.

The next morning, I put what few things I had into the Cutlass, and gathered my maps. I knew I was heading Interstate 40 west to I-10, and after that I was to call my uncles who would guide me the rest of the way. I put in my Heavy D cassette and hit the road.

Chapter 20 ~ California, USA

While walking down a slight hill it began to feel like I was being pushed by someone from behind. When I turned around, I saw my fellow classmates and friends with a look on their face. ... Then a voice came across the intercom, "This is not a drill. Take cover."

* * *

Everything at school was going great. I was learning my trade as a Yeoman and improving my people skills. I had three sets of friends at school... my black friends, my white female friends and the guys I would ball and drink with. The most difficult group was my black friends, mainly females who had all kinds of drama and always competing for each other's attention. I remembered what Chief said to me, so I had proceeded with caution with all of them.

I had finally come to grips with my sexuality. I was no longer prescribing to the fact that I could or would date a man. I was very naïve to the fact of what and who I was. I felt like because I could still be around a lot of women and not be attracted to them, that I was a special kind of lesbian. I would soon find out it was not a special trait, but something I possessed when I was dating men as well. It was called an attraction. I guess I thought by accepting the fact that I was gay, I would no longer be able to have regular female friends. Even though I had friended females all my life, I never saw myself as gay.

If I never accepted my gayness, that was fine and I wouldn't have to lose any friends. I was scared females would be afraid of me. Even if I didn't like them like that, it's what they'd think when I was around. I still moved around quietly but friendly. But these girls were a mess. There were two other females that proclaimed to be gay, one more masculine than the other who was also very polished in her communication skills of persuasion. They both actually preferred feminine lesbians. My mind was not focused on that because I was still missing Marilyn and worried about her. I was the sounding board for my two friends who often went back and forth on which of our other lady friends they'd pursue.

Petaluma was about an hour from San Francisco. I had an uncle who lived in Daly City, which was a suburb right outside of San Francisco. I spent a few days with him before I reported to school and he had asked that I return to visit again. I really didn't know him that well. I'd never really said more than hello and good-bye whenever he'd call to talk to my grandmother. He left Arkansas when I was really young, but I knew my grandmother would fly out to spend time with him on an annual basis.

He had a very impressive lifestyle and seemed to always

have money. Everyone talked about how well he was doing in California. He had an older cousin who had moved to southern California in the Los Angeles area, after leaving the service. They were like brothers. My older cousin, Steve, was like an uncle to me as well. Both of them living in California and doing so well was such an inspiration to me. I bragged about them all the time to my new friends. Uncle Steve was very close to my mom. They all had a bond and those two were very excited to have me in California, even if it was just for a few months. The only thing about my uncle in Daly City was that he drank too much and that's putting it mildly.

When I got to his apartment, in a building that I later found out he owned, he was so excited to introduce me to everyone. He proudly announced, "This is my niece. My little sister's girl. She drove all the way out here from Arkansas." All kinds of people came to the apartment to meet me and we drank and drank. I was tired after having driven all day and needed to lay down. After my uncle showed me my bedroom, I immediately fell into a deep sleep as soon as my head hit the pillow. Then I felt something close to me and I jumped up. My uncle had gotten in the bed with me. My mind immediately jumped back to my childhood, but I could tell instantly he wasn't there to hurt me. It wasn't like in a perverted way, but a sad way. I got up and asked if he was okay.

He started talking and talking about his life growing up in Arkansas and how everyone told him he wouldn't be shit. He was drunk, but he needed for me to hear his story so I listened. When we woke the next morning, I mentioned the jumping in the bed wasn't cool because I was a grown ass woman. He apologized and we laughed. We spent the day in town together. Everywhere we went people knew him, and talked about how good and generous of a guy he was. I soon realized everywhere we went he never paid for anything. Everyone was like, "It's on me. Get me next time." I asked one of his homeboys what was up with my uncle not having any money on him. His friend said, "We don't let him carry money around because some of these young cats would take advantage of him when he's had too much to drink. Don't worry. We take care of your uncle. When it's time to settle the tab we're straight with him." The guy said my uncle was too good to be used.

Before I left for school, he made me promise to return with friends. I was worried about him, but he was an artist and a sculptor. His brain was wired differently. I talked to him about his work and he loved talking about it. He kept calling me little Naomi because my aunt's name was Naomi as well. He kept saying how smart I was and that I was going places, "But little Naomi, you make sure you treat people good.

When you are good to people, they will be good to you." I promised him I'd come back for a weekend with friends. Those few days I spent with my uncles were some of the most precious days, and will forever be special to me

Here we are now, me and my friends, ready for a weekend in San Francisco. Since I was the only one with a ride it was up to me to get us there. Only six people could fit in the Cutlass. It certainly had to be me and my two mac daddy friends as we use to say back in the day. I wasn't that interested in any of the ladies romantically because my mind was still stuck on stupid with Marilyn. It didn't matter to me who went because I wasn't trying to hook up with anyone. My friends, however, had their eyes on a couple of the ladies who they thought were bi-curious. I had a straight friend who had a man back in her hometown. She was my safe bet, so I picked her. She knew about me and Marilyn and I knew about her man, so we were good to go.

My friends and I had received much attention from the ladies of the Caucasian persuasion, but we chose to take some sistas on the trip. We didn't know if we could trust them if something went down, not to mention my "May" experience. We knew the sisters would stick to the story because they weren't going to be outed like that. Even if they were straight and slept with one of us that story would never be told.

There we were in San Francisco's mecca of GAYNESS. It was the late 80's and this was like nothing I had ever seen. Never in Chicago had I gone to any gay bars. We had been to a few bars in Little Rock, but nothing like this. There were all gay restaurants, neighborhood taverns, and pool halls. We went to straight and gay bars because outside of myself and my two friends, none of the other ladies were gay. Even though they spent every minute with us, they were in relationships and had never expressed an interest otherwise. One thing my little venture into the lesbian world had taught me was to let a straight woman indicate if she was interested – anything else would be crossing the line.

We met my uncle from Daly City at a restaurant for fish. He had reserved the whole back room for me and my friends. We had all we wanted to eat and drink. We laughed and had the best time. I watched my family accept me and my friends with open arms. I think that's the moment I understood to treat people with extra care when they visited – to bring out the red carpet because they were choosing to be with you. That's what my uncles had taught me.

After dinner, my uncle said he had a gift for me. It was a Canon T90 camera in a fancy case with all the bells and whistles. As he gave it to me, he said take plenty of pictures to capture memories of my time in Cali. He reminded me that I had my mama's fight and my aunt's smarts and wanted me to cherish the time. There was a sadness in his eyes as he talked. I knew he was much more than just a country boy from Arkansas. I saw a man fighting through the pain of his past, fighting for all that he thought he was promised. He was a man who lived through art, coping with his pain through alcohol, but I also saw his soul and spirit.

I saw a little of me in him fighting to survive. I was struggling with who I was also – fighting through dreams and wants that didn't seem to fit what society said I should be and have. I wanted Marilyn in my life every day, but she was married to a man. I knew I had to find someone to replace her in my heart, but it was just not that simple. What I felt for her was different. I felt Marilyn completed me. She was the period at the end of every one of my sentences in life. She helped me to complete my thoughts. It was hard for me to catch my breath when I thought of her not being in my life. Yet, I had to find a way to replace her because she could never be my woman. She had a husband now.

We returned to school to finish up our last few weeks before finding out where our new military life would lead us. It was October 17, 1989, and a group of us were walking from the mess hall back to the barracks. While walking down a slight hill it began to feel like I was being pushed by someone from behind. When I turned around, I saw my fellow classmates and friends with a panicked look on their face. We couldn't figure out what was going on, but as we approached the barracks, we noticed pictures were shaking and falling from the walls. Then a voice came across the intercom, "This is not a drill. Take cover." We were in the middle of an earthquake and none of the girls had any idea what to do. It seemed it lasted forever, but it was really only a few seconds. We were about forty-five minutes to an hour away from San Francisco and the Bay Area, but we felt it.

When the shaking stopped, we had muster call to account for all personnel. When power returned after a minute's loss, we observed the devastation on TV. Everyone immediately started wanting to contact loved ones to let them know we were fine. But the phones started ringing and we decided every person would only spend two minutes, on the phone in order for everyone to hear from their loved ones.

The phone rang and my name was called. I rushed to the phone. It was her on the line with Alexis in the background, like all the other times she'd called. She immediately said she'd seen the news and they were scared. Alexis was really getting upset. She then said, "Hearing your voice means everything to me right now." I told her I couldn't talk long but I would call the next day to give her the details. She was relieved and would let everyone know that I was okay. Alexis spoke through the phone telling me how much she missed me and that she loved me. Before we got off the phone,

Marilyn said, "I Love you and I pray for you every night."

I didn't know what to think of that. I knew Marilyn was always a spiritual person. She knew the Bible, and she taught me how to turn to the Word in times of need. She had taught me I needed to have my own personal relationship with God. Her saying she loved me was confusing, because I knew she loved me, but I needed to accept that word of love as one from a spiritual sister and not of an enduring lover. I had to accept those words meant something different now.

The time had come to receive our first permanent duty assignments for the next three to four years. We were able to request up to three locations, but it was clear that assignments were based on the needs of the service. I chose places near Arkansas to be close to Alexis. My first choice was to return to New Orleans because I was familiar with the area.

When the instructor called my name, he said, "Wow! This is nice." My first thought was that I'd been assigned to New Orleans, so I was thinking, 'Great! I got my wish.' Then I heard "1st District Office". I thought I heard 8th district and my heart started racing. All I wanted to do was get to a phone and call Marilyn, but then I heard Boston, Massachusetts. My mind failed to connect the words coming from the instructor's mouth to my brain. "Boston?" I asked loudly. To no one in particular, I said, "Where is Boston?" One of my shipmates responded that it was in the coldest part of the east coast.

Chapter 21 ~ Boston, USA

I asked how he knew. He said, "I could pick up the chemistry. I could feel the vibe when y'all were around each other." That meant if he could feel it others could as well.

* * *

Upon my brief return to Arkansas from Petaluma in January, I was able to visit with Alexis and Marilyn, who was full blown pregnant to the tune of eight months. Soon after I arrived, it was time to head to Boston and we had a long, drawn out good-bye. I kind of felt like maybe this was the end and that we were over.

In a strange way, I felt like going to Boston was kind of a relief because it was far away enough that I could maybe start to mend and move on from Marilyn. I was excited and scared because I knew that if I was too far, that somehow might interfere with my opportunities to see Alexis. When I shared the news with Marilyn, she was excited also. She expressed a little sadness about the distance, but I sensed she felt the same as I did. Maybe it was what we both needed.

I took the drive to Boston in the Cutlass just riding freely. It was cold and I had never driven in cold weather or on ice. I was hoping to make it out east before it snowed. As I approached the Tennessee mountains, headed up toward

Pennsylvania, it started to get colder and gloomy. I was getting nervous about the possibility of running into ice. My first night, I stopped in the Smoky Mountains of Tennessee and could literally see the smoke coming off the mountains. I had never seen anything like that before. I was in awe and overwhelmed with all of the beauty of seeing something so different and unique. I was enjoying my ride out to the east. The scenery was beautiful and helped to take my mind off of the fact that I would be in Boston for the next three years.

I arrived in Boston a few months after the Charles Stuart incident. Charles Stuart was a white man that shot and killed his pregnant wife while sitting in a car. He shot himself in the leg to make it look like a carjacking. He claimed it was a black guy, so Boston police went on a manhunt. They searched and harassed young black men throughout the city looking for a suspect that didn't exist. You could still feel the racial tension in the city. I had been previously told that Boston was a pretty prejudiced town and to be careful in certain parts of the city. Whether you were black or white, there were certain neighborhoods you just didn't enter. In some ways, the segregation reminded me of Chicago.

I got situated in the barracks, started developing friendships, hanging out, and meeting people. Then the letters started coming. Marilyn shared everything that was going on and how she was doing, especially involving the pregnancy. I wrote her back often and would send letters back as soon as she wrote me. Although we had general conversations, she also expressed that she didn't know if she could continue in her marriage after she had the baby. I didn't quite know how to take that. I felt she needed a friend to talk to.

As her friend, I listened and felt I owed it to her to really try and understand where she was coming from. I also felt conflicted because as a person that was in love with her, I wondered if I needed to just be a casual friend and maybe not a best friend. Marilyn had never shared any feelings about him to me, and I, in no way, wanted to sway her in any direction, period. My letters were vague, but friendly. I didn't want to convey how I felt about the situation, but I could feel that she was really struggling with whatever was going on. She was not happy, but thought if she gave her marriage a chance that she eventually would be. She kept talking as though you were to make it work for someone you love, but she never said she loved him.

February came with great news of the new baby's arrival. Yep, she was here – the second baby of Marilyn and her husband. She kept telling me she was the sweetest baby, didn't cry, and was absolutely adorable.

I told Marilyn I'd been working on getting a mutual exchange to return to New Orleans because I wanted to be closer to

Alexis and now the new baby. I needed to get back to being a part of their lives. Boston was nice, but I wanted to be back in New Orleans. New Orleans had been pretty good for me, even after the investigation. I couldn't deny the genuine friendships I'd made with some good people. I felt good about going back there because some of them were still there. Marilyn was excited to hear that. Because I had to pay for my transfer out of pocket, I worked a second job as part of a set up and break down crew for conventions being held downtown. I also wanted to be able to send money in case she ever needed it.

One night after leaving my part-time job, I went through a yellow light. I immediately heard a siren. I was nervous about being stopped by the Boston police, especially with racial tension still being in the air. I pulled over and placed my hands on the steering wheel. I could see the officer approach my vehicle with his hand on his gun. He started yelling, "Let me see your hands!" He asked why I was in such a rush. I told him I wasn't. He asked for my driver's license and before I could say anything, he yelled about my Arkansas plates.

As I told him I was in the military, he started inching closer to the car and uttered in a sarcastic tone, "Military, huh? Well let me see your military ID." He advised me to just move slowly, as I was getting it out of my jacket. He looked in the car and inquired about boxes in the back. I informed him that I had just left my part-time job and was taking fish from the fish show to my shipmates that the crew had been given. He looked at my military ID, handed it back, and told me it was my lucky day because he liked the military. "Now get out of my face and slow down." I was shaking as I watched him go back to his squad car. I was ready to leave Boston at that moment.

The standard wait time to transfer to another unit was six months. My friend from Class A school had identified a young man from Boston who was stationed at the New Orleans district office. He wanted to get back to Boston and I wanted to get back to New Orleans. We got approved for the mutual transfer. It was just a matter of waiting and staying out of trouble. Because we both had leave time, we could start a couple of weeks early instead of waiting until June.

We started the process around the early part of May. Boston had definitely been quite an experience. I partied at some really nice clubs. At one of them I'd met and even hung out with The Marvelous Marvin Hagler. The food in Boston was spectacular. I made good money, not to mention meeting really good people who became great friends. Of course, I'd also learned a lot about my job. When I was finally headed back home to New Orleans, I took in the scenery while passing through Connecticut and back down through

Pennsylvania. It was in the springtime versus when I'd come in the winter and it was absolutely beautiful.

Since I didn't have to report until June 15th I had about a week and a half to spend time in Arkansas. I was able to visit with my grandmother and, of course, my Alexis and the new baby. This would be the first time I would meet the wonderful new little Bailey. I had heard all the stories, got all the letters, and even the pictures showing how beautiful she was.

When I got to Marilyn's, I entered through the back where the baby's room was. She was in her crib as Marilyn went on and on about how Bailey never cried. As soon as I looked at her, she began to wail, but she was still beautiful as all of her pictures. She eventually stopped crying. Looking around the house, I started noticing some things. Things looked okay to the naked eye but I detected something wasn't quite right. I asked Marilyn if everything was good, and of course, as usual, she assured me things were fine. I kept wondering if she was really in a good place, but at the time being, I had to take her word for it.

When I attempted to get water from the kitchen faucet, nothing came out. I asked if it was broken and she just responded, "Oh, no. That thing acts like that sometimes." I asked, "Are you serious? Are you telling me that it's broken? Tears formed in her eyes as she began to tell me the water was off. I said, "Well, you can't have the water off. You have a baby." I didn't want to make her feel any more uncomfortable than she already did, I said, "Let's go down to the water company and take care of this." She then told me she would rather have the gas reconnected instead of the water. To keep from making a bad situation worse, I simply said they would both get taken care of.

I brought up how she'd been writing about getting out of her marriage, but had never before shared any of this. I expressed that she should've told me about the financial struggles. I reminded her that I would always be there for her and didn't want her or the girls to suffer. I needed her to promise me she wouldn't let this happen again and not come to me. After making it absolutely clear that I'd give anything and everything I owned to make sure she and the girls were safe and not in need of anything, she stared into my eyes and said, "I know that's true and I've always known it to be true. I believe you and that's what's scary." Then she turned and walked away.

~MJ's Journey~

My life in its current state was miserable. Expecting the birth of a second child to bring magic into our marriage was absurd. Things got worse instead of better. Utilities were disconnected every month, the household atmosphere was hostile, my husband had a girlfriend and everything about us was fake and superficial. I hated everything about where I was in my head space. I often daydreamed of a life with Wilma, imagining the love, the compassion, the laughter and the peace that was always present in her company. She was good to me and good for me, but a part of me identified these as selfish feelings and thoughts. I somehow managed to convince myself that a change would come. I wasn't sure what needed to change... me, my husband, Wilma or EVERYTHING.

Everything about what I was witnessing bothered me. I now knew exactly what I had read between the lines in her letters she had written. I knew what she was saying to me, she just wasn't saying it directly. I hadn't pressed the issue because actually I knew. Yet, I couldn't take a chance of making myself vulnerable and losing myself in a wave of emotions and I couldn't have my heart crushed again. Because in her world, and mine as well, she needed to be married to this man. That's what was acceptable. That's what was expected. There was no way she could be in love with me and I shouldn't love her, at least not in the way that I did. There was no way we could pretend that we could make this work. There was no way this world or our families would be accepting of this behavior... this relationship. Whatever we were feeling was selfish. There would be no path possible to have this life together unless we did it our way. Period.

One afternoon one of my older cousins came by to visit with my grandma prior to him heading back to California. He had gotten into show business in Hollywood and Las Vegas. I always looked up to him. He constantly promised that he was gonna take me, my sister, and my best friend (you know the one that wanted to beat up Marilyn), and my other cousin to Hollywood and make us stars. We didn't make it to Hollywood but he did, so in essence, we all made it.

As he headed out the door to leave, I didn't know when I'd see him again; I ran out behind him. I'd always trusted him and valued his opinion because he was more open-minded than anybody in our family. I had never told them, and even though my sister had felt it and could see that my relationship with Marilyn was different, she couldn't pinpoint how different it was. I felt comfortable with him because he was a free spirit and would understand.

As I caught up with him, I told him I needed to talk. He said, "What's up lil' cuz?" I'm sure he could sense the nervousness in my voice as I said, "I think I'm losing my mind." He said, "Well, what are you talking about? Losing your mind?" I expressed to him how I thought I was in love with a girl and he asked, "What makes you think you're losing your mind just because you're in love with a girl?" I shared how we were brought up. His response was simple, "Yeah, I know how we were brought up, but that doesn't make you crazy. That makes you gay." I shared that I didn't think that she was gay, to which he replied, "Well, you got a problem then."

Now I had to tell him about another major issue. I told him it was somebody close to the family, damn near family really, and he said, "Uh, Marilyn?" I asked how he knew. He said, "I could pick up the chemistry. I could feel the vibe when y'all were around each other." That meant if he could feel it, others could as well. Then he said the most stunning thing in the most compassionate voice, "If you love her, let her know and leave it there. If it's meant to be, it's meant to be. If it's not, be prepared to cut it and cut it off completely because you can't linger around." Those words, "cut it off completely", resonated with me throughout the years. At that very moment, I knew that I had to tell her and tell her soon. But first I needed to make my way to New Orleans and prepare for the possibility that she felt the same.

Chapter 22 ~ The PACT

I kept telling her how this was a delicate situation. There were a lot of family involved and friends as well. It wasn't just me and... She understood that, but said, "This is between you two. There is either something there or not. You have got to put yourself out there and see if your feeling is right..."

* * *

When I returned to New Orleans, after my six months stay in Boston, things were a little different than before. I wasn't going back to my old duty station. I was headed to a district office. District offices were a little stricter and a lot more refined because we were representing the whole district, not just one unit. We represented units in the states of Louisiana, Alabama, Mississippi, and parts of Texas.

The people in the office were strange and distant, not like the people that I had started a relationship with at my previous duty station as a seaman. The office was filled with messy women and gossip-latent behavior. I knew I would be an instant topic for gossip. My friend that helped me with my exchange was there. We had gone to Class A school together. She had expressed a desire to be with me while in California, but I knew she wouldn't expose me because that would raise suspicion about her.

I didn't feel like I trusted many people in New Orleans, but Sandra was still there. We were still connected and she became my tour guide when looking for a place to live. She knew I wanted to stay on the West Bank, even though the district office was in the downtown area. I enjoyed living out there and Sandra was there also. We found a nice one bedroom apartment that I could afford. I was anticipating taking care of a woman and two children on a Petty Officer 3rd class pay – a pay that didn't contain extra for a spouse and kids. If you were married, that was an entitlement given automatically. Obviously, our situation was different.

Sandra was always curious and worrisome about how I was doing. She constantly teased me about leaving her at our previous unit by herself. We had developed a big sister/little sister relationship. She was older and much wilder. I was always the one talking her off the ledge from some emotional profanity laced attack on anyone who said the wrong thing, especially anything relating to race and her blackness. She reminded me every day how I'd put her career in jeopardy when I left. She was glad that I was back in New Orleans, but she could tell something had changed in me. She couldn't quite put her finger on it. When we would hang out together and go out, she noticed I'd get quiet and shut down. She'd had enough of my ups and downs and finally asked, "What's going on?"

When I would talk it was about Marilyn and how I couldn't imagine not having her in my life. I would go back and forth in my thoughts about asking her to come be with me. Even though my cousin told me I needed to address it head on, I kept thinking I had to get over this because it wasn't right for me to feel this way. She was married and had a family. Even though she had shared with me her concern for her marriage, it just wasn't right.

I needed Sandra to help me get past this feeling. She had suggested all kind of things for me to do, including meditation. She was a Buddhist and believed I should try it and was certain it would help me. I was still learning how to rely on my relationship with God and wasn't sure if I was worthy of one with him. She reminded me of her original statement she'd made ten months earlier, "If you're tripping over a man, another will come around the corner." It was the same thought process for a woman. "You get out there. Get back on the horse and the sky is the limit, especially here in New Orleans." But what she didn't realize was that I was never really on a horse. I had never really lived this lifestyle. I had never really engaged in my sexuality as it related to pursuing someone. How things happened, just happened in my life. I mean, I went to the clubs back in Little Rock, but I never actually approached another woman. Basically, I didn't know how to.

We started going to clubs after work and on the weekends. We found a little hole in the wall to have drinks on a regular, not too far from downtown. Sometimes they had happy hour, which were the best. There were shows, food and real cheap drinks. Funny thing is, Sandra found all our clubs. She was good friends with another lesbian woman in the military. I would tease her about how and why all her friends were gay. She made it clear that she couldn't deal with a woman, and that she loved her some male parts.

No one could openly live their life as a lesbian or gay in the military. We were a few years away from the "Don't Ask, Don't Tell" era. The pressure to remain undercover was a real battle causing a constant fear. Some thought the "Don't Ask, Don't Tell" policy would relieve that fear, but it really only put a bullseye directly on people. It was blackmail gold for some. President Clinton's intentions were honorable and for the right reason, but it put a lot of people's careers at stake.

When we would go to these clubs my game was weak. My conversations were really bad and uninteresting. I absolutely had no game at all. The things that I would talk about was not the kind of things one talked about in a club scene. I wasn't really interested in having a relationship because first of all, I was scared about somebody finding out about my lifestyle and outing me. I was just nervous and always knew that somebody could hold something over my head if I got into the wrong situation. It didn't help that Sandra shared the stories of her friend, who was dating a girl and every time they had a spat, she threatens to call her superior.

I met some interesting ladies, but never made any connections. Whenever I thought one might be worth taking a shot, there would be something that made it seem as though it was a game and all about money. Finally, after several attempts, Sandra came to me and said, "Well, you know what you must do. You just gotta tell her because as long as you go around thinking and acting like this then you're not okay, not addressing the issue. You're never gonna know if she's interested in you. Just put it out on the table." I kept telling her how this was a delicate situation. There was a lot of family and friends involved. It wasn't just me and her. She understood that, but said, "It's your life and her life? This is between you two. There is either something there or not. You have got to put yourself out there and see if your feeling is right about her. And if you think that she feels that strongly about you, then it will happen or you're going to stay in this *what if* position for the rest of your life."

Then she called me by my last name, and I knew when she did that it was time for her to be big sister. "Scales, what if this is the real one, the love of your life? Doing this here – going into these clubs and making a fool out of yourself, is not you. You were built for something else. I hear you and I see you, friend. This girl is in your core and she has your soul." Then she broke the tension because she could see me getting overwhelmed. "Plus, you have no game at all."

It was early June of 1990 and I was getting settled into my new place in New Orleans. When talking with Marilyn I shared with her my adventures of going out. Sometimes she would respond, sometimes she wouldn't. On one call I let her know I needed to talk to her when I was home again, which would be the upcoming weekend. I had made up my mind to talk to her, but I had to be prepared, so I prayed for my emotional strength. My emotional stability was always in the back of my mind. Had I held so much inside that I didn't know how to accept rejection when it was something I wanted? Was I a weak person because I had let myself be overtaken by fear? My heart was longing for acceptance and needing love. Was this a character flaw? Was I worthy of love? I'd known since I was a child, I wanted my own family because then I would love them like I wanted everyone in my family to love me. I would make them a priority, shower them with love, comforting words, and never let them feel they had to fend for themselves.

There wasn't a lot of places to go to just sit, talk and have a drink. When I made it home that weekend, we grabbed something to eat and sat on the porch of my grandmother's house. I knew what I was about to say would dramatically change our relationship forever. I told her that I needed to tell her something, but before I could get the words out, she asked if she should be scared. I asked why and she said, "Because I'm afraid of how much I think about you and how much I want to be able to love you every day."

Tears ran down my face and I felt a sense of overwhelming warmth. I replied, "I know this is not the right thing to say, but I must tell you that I can't imagine a world where you are not in it. You are my world and my source of strength to believe in something bigger and better. My life is filled with many dreams, dreams I want to share with you. My world is you. It's with you, Alexis, and Bailey. I will walk this life with you on your terms, at your speed. I know our walk is meant to be together." She started crying, shaking and putting her head down.

She looked up and said, "I love you, Wilma. I have been in love with you and have prayed about it often." I asked her had she thought about what we were doing and if she was prepared for this? She said, "I can't say I'm prepared, but I'm definitely not ready to lose you. This is not what I want anymore. I'm not happy and not in love, but merely in love with the fact of being married. I thought I had to marry him because we'd been an item for years and it was the right thing to do because we had a child together."

She couldn't shake the fact that she was crazy about me. I

told her to decide how she wanted to do this. I reminded her that I'd live life on her terms, her way, and I'd never let her down if she came with me. Before I knew it, these words came out of my mouth. "I will walk this journey behind you, beside you and in front of you. Whatever you need me to do, because nothing in this world means more to me than you and those girls."

In that moment we made the PACT. We loved each other, and knew that what we were doing would not be looked upon favorably and to some, downright sinister. We knew we were changing the playing field for our families. She struggled with her words that day because she was a woman of faith, a Christian and didn't want her girls to suffer because of her decision.

~MJ's Journey~

Prior to my conversation with Wilma about the move, I heavily contemplated on what I needed to do to remain sane. I had two precious gems, my girls, who depended on me to make sure they were my priority. I also wanted to make sure that I set the example of what they needed to see. I wanted them to know that it was always mandatory to demand respect, communication and commitment from those that owed it to them.

I convinced myself that physically staying where we were did not display that. The infidelity my husband had with a female, in my mind, was inappropriate, but who was I to make that claim? Because it was an individual that I considered a family member, I inflated the inappropriateness. But who was I to measure inappropriateness? The reality of the answers to these questions did not resonate until later in years, when I realized that I had nerves.

I constantly replayed in my mind all the hurt I had done to Wilma just to show him that I was making an "attempt" to honor his request. My attempt to adjust came with a reluctancy that was obvious. It came with blatant signs that what I was doing was not what I wanted to do. I often prayed for guidance and answers because I had a praying grandmother, a father that kept me grounded in the teachings of the Bible, and a mother that made sure I was in church 24/7. I had a responsibility to follow the "do the right thing" checklist. Although I wanted badly to be out of this societal functional existence that was unfamiliar to me, I accepted that it came with a price. I wanted to move into the comfort of societies' dysfunction and into the life and space that made sense to my heart. That's what I wanted – to follow my heart. I was tired – tired of our fights, our mismanagement of household monies, our name calling, our disappearing acts, our hostile confrontations, the drunkenness and all of our LIES. **Just tired!**

My mother and I would talk very briefly about my thoughts as they related to my relationship with my husband. She had never been fond of him and had encouraged me for years and years to direct my path of relationship building in another direction. As most mom's, she always kept me encouraged and tried to do what she thought made sense for the situation, even though she saw the writings on the wall. After Alexis was born, in spite of it all, I would often tell mama that I was determined to give the white picket fence a try. I wanted to give 100% and do all I could to make it work, but I didn't. I was not able to because I was in love with someone that was not my husband. My constant thoughts, at that time, were that this dilemma would not be if it were not such a taboo.

The moment I decided that the relocating and life changing conversation I had with Wilma needed to convert into an action plan, I began moving belongings to my mom's house. At this time, I did not know what I was going to do. The transferring of my belongings, helped me settle with my conscious that this was real. I did not know at that time what I was doing and if the move with Wilma was what I would actually do. Subconsciously, I wanted my mom and grandmother's blessings, because they were all I had in my hometown that meant enough for me to entertain any second thoughts about leaving. They had watched me ride life's rollercoaster with my boyfriend, fiancé, and now my husband through the years. They'd constantly consoled me and came to my rescue repeatedly. They supported the decision of my move. We talked about what staying local would look like and that I would be subjected to more disappointment and plenty of back and forth.

We decided we'd always fall back on our friendship. We would ride this through as friends and that included all obstacles that came our way. We would always be there for each other through hell or high water. Whether the flame flickered out of our relationship, we had a goal and now we had a mission. We were going to give these girls the opportunity that she thought she was giving them when she married their father – a chance of being the best they could be. She no longer felt that could happen in their current situation. She needed to be her best in order to be the best for them.

On June 30, 1990, I drove to Arkansas with a friend of mine, a fellow sailor from my first unit. We had become very close friends. He was a cool guy from California. I had told him I had to go home to move my friend and her kids and he immediately volunteered to go with me. Before I got him on the road with me, I needed to share what he was really getting into. I told him, "She's not just my friend, but that's the story we must stick to if you know what I mean." He wanted to know exactly what he was walking into and then let me know he was good with everything and he had my back. "You lead, and I will follow," he said.

Sandra wanted to go, but she couldn't get off duty that weekend. Dave and I drove to Arkansas pulling a U-Haul hooked to the back of my Cutlass. When we got there Marilyn immediately came running out the door saying, "I don't know how much time we have, but we must put as much as we can into the trailer and we'll take off." I didn't let anyone in my family know I was coming to town. I drove back in Marilyn's car with her and the girls and Dave followed me in my car.

We were now headed back to New Orleans and the lying game would start. The PACT was now in effect and it would guide us through many storms throughout the years, which came early and often.

~MJ's Journey~

My husband had gone on one of his escapades with his woman. I had been told a few days prior that he was going out of town. I took advantage of that information and planned accordingly. Wilma and Dave came with U-Haul in tow. I was on a mission and moving fast. My oldest was puzzled and asking questions that I did not know the answers to. She partially understood why some of these things were happening because some of the actions of her father had provoked much of this accelerated decision.

The U-Haul trailer was packed to its capacity. It was a long ride down 55, and even longer when the car broke down. The load being pulled was way too much for the hitch on the poor little Cutlass. We left the U-Haul trailer in a deserted area, and kept on pushing. Our initial six-hour drive had now turned into an eight-hour journey.

When we finally made it, I was ecstatic and scared at the same time. I knew this was a stone of faith I had stepped on that was larger than life. Settling in New Orleans forced reality to find a place in my new normal. All the emotions and thoughts were fighting each other in my heart and head. Here I was with a five-year-old and a five-month old. Had I done too much too quickly? Why did I quit my job? Is this fair to Wilma? Should I have told my husband that I was taking the girls? How the hell was I going to put this packed U-Haul in a one bedroom apartment?

Although I had lived in Atlanta, it seemed like moving from Helena to New Orleans was much more of a culture shock for this ole country girl. I soon realized that I had every reason to be in shock. It wasn't about city versus country. It was more about naivete versus maturity. On day three, the apartment manager told us that we had violated the occupancy limits for a one-bedroom apartment. He stated the children could stay, but I had to go. I knew there was no room to argue the point, especially since we were all sleeping in one room and were literally leaning the extra queen size mattress on the wall each morning to allow room to move about.

Mission number one was in full force. I had to find a bigger place while hiding from the manager. That sounded simple, but more space meant more money. The search worked in our favor and didn't last long. We moved into a two-bedroom townhouse after struggling in the apartment for three months. I was relieved that we did not get put out, or should I say relieved that I didn't. We were blessed to have genuinely kind people placed in our life. When I landed a job, the lady that babysat both girls was a Godsend. I remember constantly doing what I knew to always do and that was to pray.

I began to think that lifeline, my spiritual connection may have been disconnected because of decisions I had made. Although that is what many would have liked for me to believe, of course, I did not. I have always been thankful that my faith and my relationship with God has been unwavering and has kept me safe, sane and saved. Nothing and no one on earth could change that.

Our Two Cents

We made the decision that we could no longer live apart. Although there may have been many times we put our girls and our relationship in jeopardy, we knew what we had was real. We trusted and believed in each other and stepped out on faith. Even though we were headed down a road of lies and deception, it was the path we were forging. We made the decision that this path filled with lies would protect us and the girls. We could not let this change who we were. Some might have thought our lifestyle would have been acceptable if we had been less selfish and more traditional. For safety reasons, to enjoy and afford the girls a quality of life; we were forced into these lies. For that reason, telling the truth was not an option.

Section Four

Chapter 23 ~ Settling In

Everything we did in public was a complete contrast to who we were behind closed doors... We'd go about our day, only coming together to talk and engage as a couple at night, after everything had settled down... When the sun came up, she was her and I was me.

* * *

Finally having Marilyn and the girls in New Orleans brought a new level of responsibility and anxiousness. My new office also brought on a special set of problems. Many of the guys suspected my relationship with Marilyn wasn't what I claimed it to be. Every chance possible there was an attempt to test me. There were many offensive gestures and proposals for silence, not to mention being called dykes and bull daggers. There was a constant fear of someone calling my unit to report me. These threats came from neighbors, co-workers and anyone who saw me in uniform.

Even though New Orleans had a lot of ups and downs, nothing could prepare us for what was to come with our move to Houston. The state of Texas was very conservative. There was actually a case that involved two men who were arrested for having sex one night in September 1998. While in the confines of their own apartment, a police officer burst in and arrested them for violating a Texas law that prohibited "deviate sexual intercourse with another individual of the same sex."

Our strength, the resilience of our relationship and the PACT made were being tested beyond what we could have ever imagined. We only knew that whatever happened we would face together, even while living a lie. We were determined to survive and thrive because we had risked too much to fail. New Orleans had taught us that being together was more powerful and impactful than us being apart. The move to Houston would put a tremendous stress and burden on our relationship and even though the struggles sometimes were tough, we persevered, nonetheless.

One of those struggles was a concern with the church. I was not very knowledgeable in the Word. Even though Marilyn was still growing spiritually, she was much further than I was. It had been a major part of both our lives and she wanted to keep the girls active. In spite of her own struggles, she didn't want her guilt to fall on the girls. She often taught Sunday School with hopes they'd learn in a manner that was free of the harsh scare tactics we'd witnessed growing up. She wanted them to choose for themselves, without fear and intimidation, what to believe in spiritually. We both knew they needed the fundamental structures for developing a relationship with a higher being.

We moved to the suburbs of Houston and we were in no way

a traditional family. Everything we did in public was a complete contrast to who we were behind closed doors. It felt as though we wore a mask all the time. In public we lived individual, separate lives. We'd go about our day, only coming together to talk and engage as a couple at night after everything settled down. There were never any public displays of affection toward each other. When the sun came up, she was her and I was me.

We still did some things as a family. I coached the girls and participated in all their activities as an aunt. I picked them up from school and met all their friends as if everything was normal, but nothing was normal because we weren't telling people who we were. We'd decided we wanted to give the girls a shot and not be prejudged by the two women that were raising them. Not to mention there was still the constant fear and anxiety that had followed us from New Orleans. There was the threat of the girls being taken from her and the threat of people outing me. We were not only in a battle for our lives, but for our family as well.

I was reassigned to a small duty station in Houston where I did very well. I was the public representation for both the unit and military overall. I would give speeches, tours, and worked with hundreds of students during the week. One thing I had managed to do when we were in New Orleans was finish my education. I went to night school after my day job while working a part-time job on days I didn't go to school. I had calmed down a lot since my days in Conway and even New Orleans, which was more evident on the job.

The first thing I did when we settled in Houston was apply for a position with the United States Postal Service. We decided we couldn't continue living as we were, even with the passing of the "Don't Ask, Don't Tell" policy. I'd made E-5 ranking fairly quick in my career, but it didn't seem an E-6 promotion was in the cards, otherwise I would have continued.

My mother began to take ill and since her jobs had never been that great, she became my legal dependent through the military. I was providing for her and my family on an E-5 salary, which was okay because it afforded her better health care. She was able to get all of her medicine at the base in Illinois. I realized sending her a monthly stipend to supplement her income caused her to become more and more reliant on me. Even though we didn't always see eye to eye all the time, our conversations became regular. A lot of times her anger came through, whether it was about my brother, her job, or whoever had pissed her off that day. It didn't take much to make her angry, but that's something I was used to, even as a child.

One day as Marilyn and I were sitting in the stands watching

Bailey play in a softball game, my sister called to tell me my brother had passed. He had been sick, presumedly, from the drugs he'd experimented with over time. As he had done when he was younger, he stayed in trouble as an adult. Things had started taking a toll on his body. I was expecting this phone call because I had gone to see him less than six months ago when he was in the hospital. My mother asked me to come because she didn't feel he would be around much longer. We didn't quite know what was wrong with him, other than his body was falling apart. He was weak, frail, and literally being eaten alive. We were told AIDS because of the drug use, but the details were sketchy.

When I flew to Chicago to visit him in the hospital, my mother asked me to be careful because she wasn't sure what diagnosis the doctor was actually giving him. As I walked in the room, I saw tears running down his face. He saw me and started shaking. I didn't know what to say because I had no emotions. He whispered, "Thank you." I just stood there looking at him. His skin had turned extremely dark to the point he was almost unrecognizable. I hadn't really seen him for years because we didn't really communicate a lot – not at all to be honest. I often talked with his children. I tried to keep in touch with them as much as possible. We never had much of a relationship. It was what it was.

He wanted to thank me for all I did for his children and to apologize. I accepted his apology and told him he was more than welcome. I left that day knowing it wouldn't be long before I would get *the* call.

The day my sister called I wasn't too surprised to hear from her because it was her birthday. When she told me he had passed, I hung up and just sat there. Marilyn looked at me and asked, "Who was that? Was that about him?" I answered her and turned back to watching the game. I didn't cry. I wasn't hurt. I wasn't sad.

Chapter 24 ~ Diagnosed

I knew it wouldn't be long before she needed somewhere else to live. I was hoping she could go to my sister's home for a little bit until we figured out a plan. The time came when he did ask her to leave and this was after she had accused everyone in the house of stealing a leather jacket from her and had put on quite a scene.

* * *

My Aunt Jean mentioned to me and my sister that we needed to pay attention to my mother's behavior. She was constantly laughing in an odd way and not completing her sentences. I wasn't too concerned about the laughter as much as I was about her not completing her sentences. There could be something going on. I figured she's only 56 years old, whatever was happening, it was probably something minor. We could get it looked at, be done with it, and move on to the next thing.

This happened in 2003 while in Arkansas, which was a rare trip for my mom. She didn't go to Arkansas often. I did notice that she was laughing a bit more than usual, and she also mentioned that sometimes her co-workers would leave sticky notes to help her remember things during her shift as a CNA (certified nursing assistant). It wasn't a major thing to me at that time. After her visit to Arkansas she returned to Chicago where she'd been staying with a friend. They weren't in a relationship, but she was taking care of his grandchild because helping people is something she always loved to do.

As time passed, she started complaining that other people in the house were taking her things. I was wondering who would do such a thing and why her, but whenever I called; no one else was there. She would go on and on telling me they were doing these things to her, which started to make me nervous. I asked my sister to look into it, but she blew it off as if that's just how our mother was. She was mean and probably doing things to piss people off. I'd thought maybe she was exaggerating a bit as well.

That thought was dismissed when I called one day and an elderly gentleman answered the phone. I introduced myself and explained why I was calling. He proceeded to tell me he was glad I had called because he wanted to talk to one of Ms. Helen's daughters. He had become concerned about her behavior as well. She was basically accusing everyone who came into the house of stealing from her. He also noted that she'd been getting a little confused and would get angry when corrected. He knew it wasn't her personality because they had been friends for a while. She was never a person that threw around such wild accusations. He expressed that he didn't know if she could continue to live with him because sometimes, she would make his grandchild afraid.

I knew it wouldn't be long before she needed somewhere else to live. I was hoping she could go to my sister's home for a little bit until we figured out a plan. The time came when he did ask her to leave. She had put on quite a scene and accused everyone in the house of stealing her leather jacket.

She went to stay with my sister temporarily. I just didn't know how temporary it would be. My sister was in the process of expanding her passion of baking and cooking meals into a business. She was an excellent cook, just like my mom. Helping my sister in the kitchen kept mom busy. One day my sister sent her to the store for butter. It should have been a quick, short trip, but it took longer than expected because she got confused.

This angered my sister because she thought my mother had done it intentionally. She thought she had gone to have a few drinks and hung out with some friends, instead of doing what she was asked to do. When Helen returned, there was a heated exchange and my sister asked her to leave. This meant she now had to come to Houston.

We made arrangements for her to visit. I knew once I got her here, I wanted her to be examined by a doctor. Hopefully, she'd consider staying in Houston and get her own place. I didn't know what I was going to do when she got here, I just knew we had to do something. I had recently been approved for my disability through the military, so she was able to be my dependent again. I made an appointment with my personal care physician. It had become increasingly evident that she needed some type of assistance. She was not going to be able to hold a job because she'd become forgetful. I knew she was having a difficult time retaining information, but also figured it was from grief due to my brother's death.

We got her scheduled for a routine examination. Her bloodwork showed no abnormalities. Her blood pressure was under control. She only showed medical issues related to boils and they were checked for cancer. There were no results that required any immediate attention.

Because I mentioned to the doctor a concern regarding her memory, she wanted to do another battery of tests. She asked basic questions like the date and day of the week. My mom got some of them right, but quite a few were wrong. The doctor would immediately ask the same question again and her answers would change. At that time, the doctor recommended my mom see a doctor within their network who dealt with geriatric patients and memory loss.

I was still basically thinking whatever this is it can be fixed; it can be turned around. We'd get her some medication to get her back on track. I was and still am an optimistic person. I always believe the cup is half full. I'd never thought her memory loss pertained to anything other than just a chaotic lifestyle. I figured if we could get her disability started and have her settled in a calmer environment; things would be better. My mom had been running the streets of Chicago for years. It was time for a slowdown. Then she would have a chance to have some really good days.

We met with the geriatric doctor. While waiting in the exam room my mom realized it was another doctor's visit, which upset her. The nurses seemed to recognize her behavior change and diffused the situation quickly without incident. Obviously, this was something they dealt with on a regular. The doctor entered and started asking a lot of questions. They were simple questions like the date, her name, etc. He asked her to write a few letters in order, say a sequence of words and who was the current president. She said John F. Kennedy. I could tell she knew that wasn't the right answer when she saw my facial expression. She started to laugh after her answers, and it seemed like she was just guessing or didn't understand the question.

After the test, the doctor wanted to talk with me alone in the room. He asked my mom if she wanted some coffee or juice. She wasn't a coffee drinker, but she loved Pepsi. Since they didn't have Pepsi, she was offered other soft drinks. One of the nurses led her towards the hallway to get a drink. She was skeptical about leaving me because she didn't like to be alone around strangers if Marilyn or myself weren't present.

Once alone, he asked if I was familiar with dementia or Alzheimer's. I told him I had heard about Alzheimer, but I'd never heard of dementia. He proceeded to explain that Alzheimer was a common cause of dementia. He further explained that the second most common and aggressive form was Lewy body dementia. It caused a rapid decline in mental abilities with progressive signs and symptoms such as aggressive behavior, depression, and an increased risk of falling. He asked how I planned to pay for her care. When I advised him that I was paying for the visits already, he said I'd need something beyond out-of-pocket payments.

I couldn't quite understand what he was saying. I was in a daze. All I heard was, "She has Alzheimer's." I asked if she wasn't too young to have that awful disease, but that's why he was diagnosing it as the Lewy body. This form usually came in the early ages starting around sixty, which made him more concerned because she was younger than that. He thought maybe there had been some other factors contributing to what was happening, such as a traumatic experience that may have moved the brain. He asked how much I knew about my mother's history.

I sat there in silence, stunned, because I could not understand the words that were coming from his mouth.

Personally, I felt like my soul had left the room. I asked a lot of questions because I thought maybe he was mistaken.

We left the doctor's office and went to get a bite to eat. As we ate lunch, I looked across at her face and a sense of sadness came over me. What was making her lost and confused? I told myself that everything was going to be okay. I felt in my heart she was going to get past this thing. But for the moment, I was still in complete shock. I did not want to accept what was just told to me.

My mother had been covered under my medical when I was active, but that was no longer the case. She'd had a few concerning health issues while I was active duty, which prompted me to consider other financial options so I could be there for her. I was able to assist with her bills and send extra money whenever she asked if I had it and even when I didn't have it. I found a way because she didn't ask often. Mostly she would ask for her grandkids (my brother's kids). She was not making a lot of money and needed to work, watching her friend's grandchild for some extra cash had been a great idea.

Chapter 25 ~ A New Reality

Some poor woman had fallen in love with this monster of a man, or maybe she just needed a husband because that's what women did. This was quickly turning into a legal entanglement that I didn't have any money to fight.

* * *

I had tried my entire life up until this point to be the best daughter I could be. I had waited for her on those nights when she'd come home late from work. I had gotten in the middle of her fights, and intervened during her moments of rage that led to fights in the street and provided for her when she needed it. I had been by her side and fought with her when my brother would attack one of us. She was that woman that, in spite of her faults, remained my hero.

My life was chaotic at the time. I struggled paying our bills and keeping things afloat. I was trying to hold things together because Marilyn and I had started the process of buying a house. After spending years of renting nice houses in the suburbs, paying someone else's mortgage and building their wealth, it was time for us to have our own.

While in the military, I worked several part-time jobs to maintain our quality of life. I worked at Wendy's, delivered newspapers and worked as a security guard. There was also a period of time that I worked part-time at UPS Monday through Friday. When I started at the post office, I immediately worked the overtime list at 10 hours a day for five to six days a week. Our lives, financially, were never stable. I could never make enough money to get ahead. It was always just enough to maintain.

There I was with no money or resources to take care of my sick mom. I had nothing saved and couldn't afford the premium care she needed and deserved. I felt hopeless and quite a disappointment, but I couldn't let her see me defeated. She had other things to work on and worry about. I was determined to fix this.

When I got home to share with Marilyn what the doctor said we both wept and started praying. Our prayer was simple. All we wanted was for God to guide us in the way we needed to help her. I think we both wanted to believe this was only temporary, but knew we were entering a world that neither one of us were prepared to deal with – emotionally or financially.

We immediately started the process of getting her evaluated for her Social Security Disability Insurance. I refused to believe that it was Lewy body dementia. From the moment we left that doctor's office, I started researching and doing a process of elimination picking out the symptoms she didn't have. There were many appointments and most were during the time I'd be at work.

Marilyn had a more flexible schedule and was able to take her to the appointments. We would recap with each other after each doctor's visit, hoping somehow she'd be cured. A few times she could hear the conversations when it was time for our recap, and she'd give me this weary look. Sometimes she'd get extremely emotional, frustrated and angry, which made it more obvious just how confused she was. I was still thinking, 'Well, we'll get her some medicine and she'll be fine.'

~MJ's Journey~

Witnessing the early onset of gradual changes in Helen was not difficult in the beginning because we were convinced this was temporary and the right medical care would fix it all. On the days I took her to appointments, she was always very quiet and displayed uneasiness and a little bit of fear. Those were the times I would become concerned because none of these were traits, I had ever known her to have. I dismissed it to her being in an unfamiliar city with an unfamiliar person. My biggest concern during the medical visits was not knowing the right answers to the doctor's questions. That could possibly mean incorrect information given, which could halt her recovery since there was no guarantee that she'd know the correct answer either. This was a tough period for us, but even tougher for Helen.

When we went to the Social Security Office, they realized my mother had been married. In fact, her and Hank never divorced. That meant she was entitled to his Social Security benefits if they could locate him. He'd had an excellent job with one of the automobile companies, but from the information gathered, it was discovered he was deceased. He had never mentioned or officially written that he'd been married before, so his current wife was receiving his benefits. My only thought was hoping this wife didn't have any kids. Some poor woman had fallen in love with this monster of a man, or maybe she just needed a husband because that's what women did. This was quickly turning into a legal entanglement that I didn't have any money to fight. I was trying to get my mother well, if she was to get approved it would have to be based upon her past incomes. Unfortunately, mom was the textbook definition of the "working poor" who never stayed with a job for a long period of time.

During the same process, they wanted to get all of her records from Illinois. They needed anything regarding her medical, physical, and mental history. She was able to share with them that she had been seen through Cook County Hospital. They received the few reports she had through the military, which were mainly about her medications for blood pressure.

I was eventually able to take my mom to one of her

scheduled appointments. That is when I learned she had spent a few days at Cook County's psychiatric unit. Not only did she have a few physical ailments, she had some mental issues that we'd not been aware of. We had always considered it her personality. I was actually relieved because I felt this was a chance to fix her. I thought if it was mental, we just needed to get medication to get her back on track.

It wasn't that awful thing that doctor was talking about. It wasn't this dementia thing. She was just confused because she wasn't thinking right. Yep! It was not what he said. After we got those records, they made her an appointment with a mental health physician. I was able to make a few of them and I'd sit in the hall, trying my best to hear. There'd be moments of silence and then it would get loud with the doctor trying to calm her down.

After many of these appointments, they decided to give her medicine because they thought she was exhibiting signs of schizophrenia based upon her records from Cook County. She started the medicine and I could see a change in her. She started calming down a bit, but was still getting more and more confused. Then she started hallucinating. I wanted them to take her off the meds, but of course, I was not in control. I had no real voice in this process. She was still capable of making her own decisions, but she also wanted to get off the medicine.

They'd been medicating her as a mental patient, but it was counteracting against her dementia. They put her on some other medicine that was not as harsh and it was working for her. They prescribed Aricept for cognitive impairment to help with her forgetfulness. I was convinced we were on the right track. We saw slight improvement and the medicine seemed to be making her a little more functional. She wasn't as paranoid and seemed to retain things a little better.

It was becoming very obvious she didn't want to stay in Houston. She had complained that it wasn't Chicago and was too quiet. She wanted to hear police sirens and gun shots. Those were what made her feel at home. After going through the long and arduous social security benefit approval process, she received a large sum of back pay. She felt she was independent enough to go back to Chicago and take care of herself. She expressed she didn't have to live with anybody and knew how to take her medicine. She was proud of herself and even talked about wanting to give money to my sister and grandkids. I could see her joy and sense of pride coming back. My mom was only 56 and still had a life to live. I didn't want to hold her back.

I agreed to her returning to Chicago and committed to pay her bills from the money she received monthly. In the meantime, we had this large sum of money to use towards an apartment and to get her back on track. As long as she was taking her medicine, she was functioning well. We were slowing things down. She was becoming a little more normal and back to herself with a little less hostility.

She had been responding well with her appointments and taking her medicine because she saw this as her opportunity to get back to Chicago. We would give her morning meds before we left or at least make sure she had taken them. We had great neighbors who were like family and they always kept an eye on her.

After five months with us, she returned to Chicago where she'd still have family to care for her. My sister, her grandkids, and my sister-in-law were there, so we figured she would be fine. We sent half of the back pay money to my sister for her furniture and we kept half to put towards her rent. Now that she was approved for disability and social security, she also qualified for Medicaid.

My mother didn't fly, which meant we had to find a way to get her back to Chicago with as little interruption as possible. A bus ride would be too long, with too many stops from Houston, so I drove her to Dallas and she took the bus back from there. Once she'd made it back safely, my sister helped to get her food stamps and other additional assistance. I was grateful and thankful because up until this point I had not equipped myself properly to make life better for her.

She had a boyfriend prior to coming to Houston, who she had been dating since my brother's death. He had witnessed her decline and now he would be there to see her recover. He was much younger than her, and I think he underestimated the severity of her memory problems. He never connected the dots and it made me think that maybe he thought there were other contributing factors to her behavior. I thought he was taking advantage of her because she was a very generous person. If she had anything, she would share it with the masses. When she returned, they reconnected and he moved back in with her. I was okay with that in the beginning because it's what she wanted. As time went on, he wasn't really helping her. He wasn't there much and he was not prepared for her. She wasn't taking her medicine every day, and eventually she stopped taking it altogether. He bailed after that.

Soon after she would call every day and ask if I'd sent her money. Every day I would tell her it had already been sent or it wasn't time yet. Every day she would wait on the mailman. She'd tell them I was supposed to send her money, that her daughter in Houston had her money and was stealing from her. She asked the mailman to call me one day from her phone, and he did because he was worried about her.

In most cases, we (letter carriers) were the one face that many people saw every day. Talking to them would help to put a face and a life behind the name on the envelope. Sometimes you would meet that one special person or persons that just grew on you. I would take time with my customers every day, especially the elderly ones. There was one I had a couple cups of coffee with every morning and the husband would scratch off his lottery tickets. Then there was Ms. Hernandez. She was my favorite and would ask me to read the mail she deemed important. She thought I could catch maybe something she or her sons might have missed. She just needed someone to spend a little extra time and remain fully engaged with her. This reminded me a lot of my mom.

I was not surprised when he called me. As a matter of fact, I was proud of my fellow letter carrier. I'd started to get concerned about my mom. My Aunt Jean sent a letter voicing her concerns to me and my sister. She felt we needed to be more present in my mom's life because of the things she was saying. In my mind, I had done my part. I was instrumental in getting her evaluated and she was on the road to recovery. I had totally accepted that the doctor was wrong about the dementia diagnosis. I'd witnessed her turnaround, but was also still focused on the fact that she was only 56 years old.

My sister would take my mother her groceries, but nobody was actually going up to the apartment to check on her living conditions. We needed to know how she was doing every day. Finally, the one day my nephew went to check on her, he said she had removed all the plates from the light switches and thought that she really shouldn't be staying there by herself.

Chapter 26 ~ Storm

I was terrified of the news being shared from the other end. When Wilma told me what had taken place, my heart sank.

* * *

The phone rang at 3:00 am. It was the Dallas police. They had located my mom and placed her in Parkland Hospitals' psych ward. There had been a disturbance at the train station. Apparently, she was acting irrational because she was lost and afraid. All her demons, fears, and pain surfaced at a time when she could not find the words to express her confusion.

I knew this phone call was not just to notify me of a disturbance. Instead, it was a wake-up call to the reality of my mom's decline – a woman I had simply adored my entire life. My mother was starting a journey in her life that would sadden and strengthen me at the same time. The progression of my mother's illness was starting to take control, things had finally come full circle, and I could no longer deny or have wishful thinking that it would go away. There was no miracle care. There was no miracle pill. I was not prepared mentally, financially, or in any way. One might even say I was almost reluctant because I felt like I had done what I thought I was supposed to do. It was too soon for me to think about the care of my mother, who by this time, was only 57 years old. I had done my part and had gotten her back on track. I'd sent her home to Chicago where she wanted to be in familiar territory with family and friends to assist. I had done my daughterly duties, but she was now back in Texas.

When the police called, I was nervous and didn't know what to expect to hear from the other end. When I answered, they called me by name and asked if I knew a Helen Brown. I informed them she was my mom. He then identified himself as being with the Dallas police department.

Even before receiving the call from the officer, I knew something was wrong because when I went to meet her at the station for her scheduled arrival to Houston, she didn't get off the train. I immediately started calling around to places that I thought she might have traveled through on her return from Chicago. I called Amtrak in Houston and Dallas, as well as both Greyhound stations. I tried filing a missing person's report, but wasn't allowed because she had not been missing the required length of time. I did activate a senior citizen medical alert in the city where I thought she might be. Since Dallas was the only stop on her trip, I made the call to the Dallas police.

The plan was to have her return by train because it would only be one stop with no layover. My sister made sure my contact information was placed everywhere possible on her person. However, here's what I think happened.

She was sent by train with plans to switch in Dallas. When she was asked to detrain, she ended up at the bus station with a train ticket. Understandably so, because the two stations were close together. The customer service rep kept telling her that she had a train ticket, but she was persistent on it being the bus because that is how she usually traveled. Since she had not been taking her medication on a regular, she was confused and anger took over. What they saw was an out of control woman causing a scene. Unaware of her condition, they called the police who took her in for disorderly conduct.

After having called around all night a connection was finally made. They realized they had someone in a holding cell that needed medical attention. The police informed me that my mom had been taken to Parkland Hospital. My information had been found on her and I needed to get in touch with the hospital. I was in Houston and Dallas was every bit of a four-hour drive. I contacted my sister and told her I had located mom and that she was in Dallas. My sister had a friend in Dallas who she asked to go be with her until I could get there. When I got off the phone, Marilyn was staring at me with tears in her eyes. I laid my face into the pillow and cried. An immense sense of sorrow took over me. I was relieved she was okay, but now I was scared because I didn't know what condition she was in. Panic and anxiety took over and I felt sick. Marilyn held me in her arms. She assured me that whatever happened, we were in this together, that my mom needed to remain with us, and everything would be okay.

~MJ's Journey~

I was terrified of the news being shared from the other end. When Wilma told me what had taken place, my heart sank. I could not begin to imagine what Helen was going through, but also the emotions Wilma was experiencing seemed inexplainable. I remember holding Wilma as tight as I could and desperately trying to convince her that since Helen was safe, everything would be just fine once we got her home. At the same time, I was asking myself, 'Will it really?'

When I called my supervisor at work, I explained what had taken place. She was aware that I was dealing with a stressful situation with my mother and was very compassionate. That was a rarity because usually a family emergency meant nothing to certain post office supervisors. I headed to Dallas driving like a maniac, arriving in three hours.

At the hospital, Tancy, my sister's friend, was sitting next to my mom as she laid in her hospital bed. Tancy was talking with her and trying to make her remember who she was. Walking into that room and seeing someone that had my mom's best interest at heart was one of the greatest feelings to have at such a tough time. I was immediately overcome with a great sense of relief. I could not thank her enough. Tancy just wanted to comfort me and make sure I was okay. When I saw my mom, she recognized me. I could see in her face that she had been through pure hell. I kissed her on her forehead and jokingly said, "Woman you are hardheaded."

Even though my mom was sick, she was never a person that would accept anyone feeling pity for her and I definitely was not going to make her feel like she was helpless. I just wanted to assure her that I would be by her side. Tancy invited us to spend the night at to her house. I told her I needed to take my mom home and get her settled. There were no words to express my gratitude to Tancy because she had no obligation to go and be there for me. At that moment, I felt lost. Although I loved my mother dearly, acts of affections were not common in our family relationships. I had to trust and believe that she knew I loved her and that my heart was hurting. I needed her to know that I was that tough little girl she had taught me to be, even though I wanted to roll up in a ball and lay down next to her and cry my eyes out. When we were leaving, the staff was wonderful and full of compassion. It felt as though there was a village wishing me well and wanting the best for my mom. I was strong every minute I was in my mother's presence, but with the staff I was an emotional wreck.

On the ride back from Dallas, I stared at my mother, as I reflected on our life in Chicago and all the things we had gone through. I shook my head in amazement. The four of us had seen and gone through so much together. Here we were, my brother dead at the age of thirty-seven and my mom diagnosed with dementia at fifty-seven. She slept most of the ride back to Houston. They had given her medication to calm her down. She was quite tranquil, but looked frazzled. She would talk for a minute, then fall right back to sleep. She looked tired, but not defeated. Somehow, I still saw a bit of grit and spunk.

As I looked at her, anger took over. I was angry at myself. I knew I had to do something different. I had been afforded plenty of opportunities in my life, more than she had ever had. I had experienced great paying jobs with excellent benefits, was educated and needed to do something to change my family fortune. I needed to be the person that I had always dreamt of being. It was my duty to be the best I could be for my family. On the drive back from Dallas, I made the decision to begin to live that fantasy life I wanted, that life that no one could tell me didn't exist. I had lived it every day in my head as a child. It was the life I always told my girls about.

I often told myself they were not victims and would not be a statistic. They would have the opportunities as all others from "traditional" families. I was convinced that I needed to take advantage of the fact that things were better for me than for my mom. I had not taken advantage of all that I could have. I had completed college and wasn't using my education, but totally indebted to the student loan program. I was content with not using the tools that I had struggled to achieve. Had survived the projects, the streets of Chicago and overcome sexual abuse from within the walls of my own home, at the hands of those who were to take care of me. I survived battles of mental instability, lack of confidence, a near death experience and had avoided the pitfalls that so many I knew had succumbed to, such as drug and alcohol abuse. I needed to look at my blessings and recognize that I had been given a lot more than many and needed to do something with it. It was in this moment I decided I would change my focus and switch the approach I was taking regarding the care of my family. But for now, I had to get my mom home and convince her that she was safe with us.

When we made it home, Marilyn had cooked a full course meal for her. As she ate, I could see the fear in her eyes. All I could do was imagine what she had gone through. She couldn't tell me everything because she couldn't remember much about her trip. It was apparent that my mother's health had declined. She was much more confused and extremely paranoid. Marilyn had prepared the extra bedroom for her and I made her bath water. She was welcoming my attention and wanted my affection... something she had never shown before. I had never seen my mother's body and thought it would be years before I would be faced with being her caretaker. I knew the things required to care for an elderly parent because for years Marilyn and her siblings had been sharing that responsibility in the care of her mother. Marilyn's mother was much older than mine. As a matter of fact, she was old enough to be my mom's mother.

~MJ's Journey~

When they returned from Dallas, I was nervous about the meal I had prepared. Helen was a great cook and cooking for someone that does it well is challenging. She appeared detached and distant, but seemed to enjoy the meal. With all the experience I had preparing meals, bathing and caring for my mom, doing these things for Helen was different. It was different because this was not where she was supposed to be. I remember watching Wilma do the things for her 57-year-old mom that I would do for my then 83- year-old mom. Although they both had a form of dementia, Helen's was such an early onset of it and it was obvious that it was definitely a different level of memory loss. My mom's dementia mimicked old age senility as opposed to Helen's loss of memory being associated with paranoia, rage and distrustful behavior.

As I washed her back, I saw in her eyes that this incident had damn near broke her spirit. My emotions were mixed with anger and sadness. My mom was being robbed of a quality life. From this day forward, I would be her voice. I had to be the stabilized force in her life now. I needed to be the best me and anger was not going to allow that. It had always brought the absolute worse out of me and would take me to a place of rage. The care of Marilyn and the girls required me to be strong, stable, and not consumed with anger like it had been in the early years of life. I had grown spiritually and emotionally, but my heart was now broken because my mom, the first love of my life, my hero, the person that knew everything about me and that my life with Marilyn was one of real love was now sick... really sick. This was extremely difficult for obvious reasons, but also because she loved me unconditionally and always kept my secrets. She had encouraged me to love who I loved and to do it in style. I needed my mom to trust me – something she didn't do much. She was extremely tired, she slept for two days, only waking to eat.

I started researching and studying this disease again. I needed to know what to expect. After reading various pieces of material, brochures and books over and over, I finally accepted the fact that she had Lewy body dementia because she had all the symptoms.

It was driving me crazy to read this over and over and none of the risk factors pertained to her. Lewy body dementia had three common elements: age, sex and previous family history. Regardless of the initial symptoms, over time, all factors of Lewy body dementia would eventually affect one's cognitive, physical, and behavioral state, and even sleep.

I kept reading about the complications and the words "progressive" and "Parkinson" were often mentioned. I knew I needed to be familiar with the stages of dementia and Alzheimer, so I closely examined each phase, while praying that a cure would be found before she reached the next stage. I had made up this imaginary timeline and convinced myself that I would have her healed. If nothing else, it would give me time to work on my plans for gaining additional revenue and improving my financial affairs before she would need 24-hour care.

I decided and formulated in my mind that I needed a source of income that would significantly change the trajectory of my family's wealth, especially with my mother being sick. I needed to be in a better position to help her, but more than anything I needed to live up to all the wild dreams I had as a child. The dream of having a family, a business and doing any and everything I possibly could think of. Now at the age of 40, everything was thrust in my face. My mom now had what I think she had been seeking all her life. She had someone totally committed to her and her well-being. She finally had someone who cared about her and was no longer in this tailspin of misguided and unfortunate love triangles because often her relationships were one-sided. They were not all bad, but many were, and I couldn't help thinking that some were responsible for us being where we were.

She was back in Houston in our new home – the house where she sat for the closing, witnessing her baby girl's dream come true with the love of her life. This was as much her house as it was ours as she had gone on the many visits with us looking. She probably didn't remember it all. Even still, she didn't want to live with us. She wanted her own, but we couldn't take a chance on what happened in Chicago happening here. My mother was not capable of staying by herself.

Our lives were busy. I worked all the time, coached basketball, and spent my evenings reading and researching. We had a kid in college and it was by the grace of GOD, because it's not like we had financially prepared for her to go. This was not like when I went to school. There were no grants and if there was any free aid, we didn't qualify because Marilyn made too much money.

Alexis was returning to the place where she had spent five years as a child. Since we were ill prepared to send her to college, I needed to turn to my Aunt Jean for her help. Education was everything to her, she was an educator and wanted all her nieces and nephews to go to college, even if the adults in their lives where too dumb to prepare. My family struggled tremendously with Marilyn and my relationship because we never faced it or addressed it head on with them. We were hell bent on protecting the girls from ridicule and people treating them different. We were blinded by the fact that we were denying anyone to see the love that was present in our home. It was obvious that Marilyn and I had real chemistry. It only took a couple of minutes to notice it when you are in our presence. Even though we didn't care what people thought of us, Alexis' father was like a brother to my aunt. This was all a serious family entanglement.

I knew my mom wanted her own independence, but we had to manage it. How could she be independent, what if she forgets things like to turn the stove off. I studied the stages and was keeping track of her progress of this disease. There are seven stages and I used this as motivation to get right with my finances and my plan.

We figured she could go to a community of people similar to her at the stage she was in now. She could be independent, could come and go and would have her own apartment. There was a place around the corner from the house. Marilyn and I paid them a visit. It was nice and well maintained, but as we toured the facility, we saw the residents were mobile and active. We also noticed that most of them were white, which I knew would be a problem for my mother. The biggest problem, however, was the cost.

Based upon the income she was receiving from Supplemental Security Income (SSI) for her disability, Marilyn and I would have to contribute at least $4500 a month of our own money. We could not afford that. What in the world were we going to do? We figured we would search closer into the city for affordable facilities since we were in the suburbs. My Aunt Jean, Helen's big sister, offered to help in any way she could. Of course, my Uncle Steve made it clear, also, that he was just a phone call away. This was very difficult for both of them, because they were losing their little sister. As much as I was hurting, I couldn't imagine how this was affecting them.

Unfortunately, my mom started to take on a lot of the traits that a small group of Lewy body dementia patients have, which are the neuropsychiatric symptoms such as: hallucinations, behavioral problems, and difficulty with complex mental activities. We'd have these heated discussions and she would call me all kinds of names. I knew it was the sickness and never took it personal. Until one day when we were standing in the kitchen and she was hounding me about her cigarettes or money – I don't know which because she constantly accused me of stealing from her. On this day, she decided to tell me that I was nothing but a bull daggin' dyke. My feelings were hurt, but I knew it was the sickness. Yet, it didn't stop me from saying, "That's okay. But you only gonna get one time to call me a dyke and then we gone have a problem." She looked at me and I think she knew what I meant. Hell, I didn't know what I meant, but I would never hurt my mom. I think she sensed my body language didn't agree with her comment. She also knew the apple didn't fall far from the tree. Just like she didn't take unnecessary BS, I didn't either. I never heard those words from her mouth again.

We did find her a place in the city with people more around her age and color. I took her there, but didn't feel comfortable. It didn't look as nice as the other one, but my mom was happy. It was a home for adults who needed little attention and someone to help monitor their medicine. They were allowed to smoke cigarettes, so she felt right at home. Because the place was not too far from my job, I would go by there every day after work. Every day only lasted for three days when one day after work I went to visit and just didn't like it anymore. It wasn't clean and I didn't want her there. I told the lady that mom would be going home with me and never to return.

I had to lie to her to avoid a scene because she wanted to

stay. I told her that I wanted her to come home to have dinner with me. She agreed and when we got home, she never asked about returning. She went upstairs after dinner and went to sleep. But that would only last for a day because she wanted to go back to her place.

Chapter 27 ~ Stage 5

She would never forgive me for that. She had worked at one of those places and I think that was one of her biggest fears.

＊ ＊ ＊

Even though my mother didn't return to that location, she still needed and wanted something of her own. She was not at the point where she needed full-time care, so we continued our search for a place that offered minimum supervision. It was obvious the disease was progressing as I'd read in my research. I thought we had found a place that was perfect for patients at this stage in the disease. They locked the facility at night to prevent the patients from wandering off, but they still had the freedom to move around during the day. We had not observed her wandering off. Although she would become quite restless and get up during the night and walk up and down the hallways of the house. She also started experiencing more of the hallucinations, especially right after taking her morning meds.

We had gone to several locations while also trying to find the right medicine to work with the meds she was taking to slow the progression of the memory loss. Some of the visits required her to stay a few days to be evaluated, but she always returned home. It was like some of the doctors were treating her for two different medical conditions.

We finally found a place where she could be somewhat self-sufficient and feel like she was on her own. We were relieved because it gave her a sense of autonomy. I could call anytime, go by and see her anytime and that made me more comfortable. Whenever she'd go out during the day, she'd be with fellow patients. However, one morning I called to see how she was feeling and to remind her I would be coming by after work, no one could find her.

They went to her room, but she wasn't there. They assured me she was still outside. I nervously waited and called back an hour later and she still wasn't in her room. I felt very uneasy about the whole situation. I could feel it in the pit of my stomach, something wasn't right. They told me she went out every day and always came back with the others. They kept telling me not to worry, that she was fine. But the second time I called, they informed me she didn't come back in with the others. I freaked out and started asking how this could happen.

I left work immediately. I told my supervisor I had to go because my mom was missing. I told Marilyn I was headed over there. Marilyn said she would meet me, but I told her to stay home just in case she came that way. When I got there, they had been looking around and questioning the other residents she went outside with. One of the residents told them she had gone to look for her daughter. He thought she was okay. He didn't worry about it because she would always go looking for her daughter and always return. My jaw dropped to the floor when they told me that. Then the nursing staff wanted to scold me because they felt like I knew she was a wanderer. I told them she'd been there for two weeks and had never wandered, plus she never wandered at home. It was obvious they were trying to make sure I wouldn't blame them for her being missing. This conversation was starting to get very heated when the nurse told me she had been a little aggressive with some of the residents and they couldn't have that. I couldn't believe they wanted to have this conversation right then while my mom was lost. It was very apparent that she was trying to convey to me that my mom couldn't return.

I drove around the neighborhood looking for her, got out of my truck and walked the surrounding neighborhoods. In the midst of their attempt to cover their asses they informed me they had contacted the police to make them aware of her disappearance. Nightfall hit and still there was no sign of my mom even after canvassing the entire area. Upon my return to the facility, there was a police car sitting outside of the building. As I got closer, I noticed Marilyn's car was there as well. My mother was in the back seat of the police car. She recognized me immediately and smiled as if she was relieved. She then said to the police, "There she is," referring to me. "We found her," she said. All I could do was smile because I was about to pass out from panicking and worrying. Seeing her face put air back into my lungs.

Marilyn had come because she couldn't just stay home; she wanted to look for her. Bailey was home sitting by the phone. Marilyn had seen her in the car and tried to explain that she was her daughter as well. The police told her they could only release her to me because I was her legal guardian. When she got out of the car Marilyn and I both rushed to hug her. She looked surprised as if she didn't understand why we were so happy to see her. In her mind she had been looking for us.

Marilyn and my mother had a very special relationship before she got sick. They didn't meet eye to eye all the time, but they respected each other very much. Sometimes they would have very candid conversations, which sometimes made me nervous, but they would always end with mutual respect. Since my mom's move to Texas, Marilyn had spent a lot of time with her and really appreciated my mom's sense of humor and her relentless determination to try and remain independent. Marilyn also enjoyed watching my mom get after people before she got sick. They had a couple of heated conversations as well. My mom always thought Marilyn was spoiled and would call her a prima-donna and Dr. Spock because she felt like Marilyn had all the answers to everything even if she didn't. I will never forget when she first said that to her. I couldn't do nothing but laugh.

~MJ's Journey~

The day that Helen wandered off, I didn't say it, but I thought the outcome would be the absolute worse. I was relieved when I saw her in the police car grinning as though I was the one that had been lost. I loved my special relationship with Helen because in many ways we were a lot alike. She didn't mince words and was always very blunt. I never took offense to her calling me a prima-donna or Dr. Spock because I knew those were her terms of endearment for me.

Marilyn wanted to know if my mom could ride home with her. I think she knew I had reached my emotional threshold for the day. She knew I needed to ride home by myself to gather my composure. When we got home, we immediately noticed that my mom was not moving like she had been in the past. After dinner, we all went to bed and I laid on the edge of the bed with my head hanging to the side. I needed to be able to see her doorway down the hall just in case she started wandering. She did get up and headed downstairs. When I heard the front door open, my heart skipped a beat. I jumped up, ran downstairs, and gently helped her back to bed.

The next morning, Helen came downstairs with several layers of clothes on. It looked like she had put on every piece of clothing she owned. She would get angry if anyone tried to tell her something different from what she was doing. This meant we had to always watch her. I asked a lady that was our neighbor from our previous subdivision to sit with her during some of our work hours. We also enrolled her in one of the adult daycares. The van would pick her up twice a week. Most mornings Marilyn had to argue with her about getting in the van. We constantly received reports from the director about her challenging behavior. The daily routine for her was getting harder and harder. Finally, one day our former neighbor informed us she couldn't continue to sit with her anymore. She felt like we were doing Helen a disservice. She told me, "Baby, your mom needs someone to be with her 24 hours a day. Ms. Helen needs to be taken care of and deserves to receive the proper attention required."

Marilyn also informed me she'd had an altercation with one of the van drivers because they told her that we were fools. They expressed the program was not for people like her. I didn't know what to do. I didn't want her to go to a place where she would be taken care of by strangers and I felt she didn't want that either. She would never forgive me for that. She had worked at one of those places and I think that was one of her biggest fears. But she started getting worse and officially entered stage 5 of this disease.

For her to receive the proper care she needed, I had to find a place with more stability. It would only be for the weekdays. I told myself that could work and we could have her home on the weekends. Marilyn agreed, which helped with the emotional part of the decision because I didn't want to be that person that put their mom in a facility. Since it would only be for the weekdays, I didn't feel as guilty. But that was not our biggest problem. We began our search, again, for a place. Each time we found an acceptable option, however, upon review of her record they became aware of her violent history. Since she wasn't bedridden, they were not equipped for someone her age and mobility who could possibly harm other residents. I was getting desperate and time was approaching when our neighbor would no longer be able to come to the house.

I contacted one of the mental health facilities where she had been before. It was one of the best places in Houston for geriatric care, but it was not a place for long-term care. This was the original place that diagnosed her as bi-polar and actually prescribed the proper medications. I wanted to know if she could just come for a short period, but the lady I spoke with was clear they had done all they could do. Fortunately, she did recommend a place down south, closer to Galveston. South of town was good for me because that was much closer to us. We had been all over the city of Houston and had been unsuccessful in finding a place closer, suitable, and affordable.

She informed me they would ask about her violent history, so there was no guarantee if they would accept her. But she felt this new facility was better equipped to handle someone like my mom. She told me to ask for the Director by name. She didn't want me to get my hopes up too high, but she felt good about it and would let them know just how wonderful of a person I was. She would assure them that this wouldn't be a "drop off and never see that family again" situation. She said it was obvious this had taken a toll on me. She respected me and my 'friend' for how much time and effort we put into my moms' care. She understood why we had fought hard to get her on the right track because my mom was so young. It just didn't make sense and wasn't fair. She further expressed since she was finally on the right meds, she deserved a chance at a good life before her time was up. I knew what she meant by "before her time was up". She was in stage 5 and from my research, this type of progressive dementia had a seven to nine year life expectancy from the onset of the disease.

It was at that point I realized that Marilyn and I had not just been dealing with a parent suffering from dementia, we had been dealing with a parent battling multiple diagnoses. My mom had been sick for years with bi-polar and even schizophrenia. She was at a time in her life when she was supposed to be enjoying her golden years. Instead, she was suffering from dementia. We had been on the battlefield together fighting an unseen enemy only to now enter a place and time where neither of us would ever be the same again.

Chapter 28 ~ Promises Made, Promises Kept

When I got on the elevator and the door closed, I let out the biggest scream because my soul was hurt. I felt like I'd let her down. I fell to the floor sobbing. The elevator door opened and a nurse got on.

* * *

Throughout this journey, I'd spent hours of researching, going to countless doctors' visits, and in and out of hospitals getting her evaluated. Now I was here. I was faced with the one thing I never wanted to do. It no longer mattered that I was preparing a plan to make things better for her financially.

It was November 2007, just a few days before Thanksgiving. We were supposed to travel to Arkansas, but the facility in Texas City wanted to meet with me and mom for a family interview. They had a room and wanted to see if this could be a good fit. Marilyn wanted to cancel the trip and go with me. I needed to do this myself. I needed my mom to know it was me and only me doing this. I didn't want her to be angry with anyone but me. I couldn't take a chance of her being mad at both of us. Marilyn and the girls left for Arkansas. My mom and I stayed home. I didn't sleep at all that night because I was nervous about the visit.

When we met the director, she was cordial and very

business-like. I immediately noticed that the residents and the staff were very diverse. I got excited and I felt in my heart this was it. While sitting in the director's office, one of the nurses came in and asked if my mom wanted to walk around. She didn't want to go at first, but agreed when the nurse told her about the snacks and drinks. When the director looked at Helen's records, she made a sigh and then said, "She has a history." I looked at her and I literally started to beg. I asked her to please give her a chance. As I was begging, one of the nurses came in and placed her hand on my shoulder. She then told the director, "We can put her on the other side where the people are more mobile. She will fit right in because we have some characters over there." The director looked at her, then turned to me and said, "Looks like she has a home." She gave me a few forms, asked that I complete and bring them back when I returned with her tomorrow. There was also a list of things to bring and what was and wasn't allowed. I just closed my eyes and bowed my head. Now came the hard work.

I didn't pack a lot. I figured I would gradually bring things. The next day my mom was excited for the car ride. When we got there, she started looking a little confused. When we got on the elevator, she started saying she wasn't staying here. I told her we were just visiting for now, so let's check it out. After meeting everyone and seeing her room, I was fine. I took her back out to go to the store, I was trying to make it as normal as possible because it was our new normal. I stayed with her all day until it was time for bed and all guests had to leave.

As I got ready to leave, she got ready too. One of the nurses saw what was happening and came in to ask Helen if she wanted to dance. I had told them how my mom loved to dance and loved music. My mom looked at me and said, "Okay, but I will see you later." As she walked away, I knew this was her home now. I would miss having her with me every day, but I had to trust that they were going to do right by her. I would definitely make sure.

When I got on the elevator and the door closed, I let out the biggest scream because my soul was hurt. I felt like I'd let her down. I fell to the floor sobbing. When the elevator doors opened a nurse got on. She pulled me up and gave me the biggest hug and told me I was doing the right thing. "Your mom is at the right place. We got her." She asked me to promise her that I wouldn't stop coming to see her because that's what she saw the most. She said, "If you promise me that, then I promise you, we got her sis." I promised her I would never ever let my mom not know she had someone here for her. I returned the next day to spend Thanksgiving with her. We had dinner and watched TV. It was bittersweet.

During this entire process of my mom's search for help, and finding a sense of peace in her journey through this, I never forgot the conversation I had with myself on the ride from Dallas. I continued to search for possible avenues of additional income for our family. I needed to know what direction I wanted to go with our new business venture. I compiled a list of books that I read. The first thing I had to do was change my mindset. I had to get myself ready to think that everything I did from this moment on would be purposeful. I always needed to be in the mindset of continuous growth and learning. I had to change how I thought about money and wealth. Wealth was beyond monetary gains. I needed to approach my pursuit of riches and wealth in the same manner in which I approached the one thing that I felt I had an abundance of, love from my family. That had to start with the commitment I made to my mom. This had to start with keeping my promise to her and myself.

Marilyn and I decided we were going to be very present and involved in her care at her new home. We visited her all the time. Marilyn would visit during the day on her lunch hour or sometimes take vacation time. She would go to lunch with her two to three days a week. Many times, Marilyn would take mom to one of the restaurants in the area, or just sit with her while she ate. I would go in the evening after work, at least four to five days a week. It just became a part of our daily routine. We didn't plan or talk about it much, we just did it. She returned home with us practically every weekend and we'd eat dinner, hang out and watch TV.

~MJ's Journey~

Placing a loved one in a facility for care is one of the hardest decisions one has to make. Knowing that Helen had to be placed as a permanent resident in a convalescent facility was very hard to digest. Hard to accept for obvious reasons, but also difficult because she appeared to be the youngest of those living in her wing of the unit. I think she enjoyed my visits with her as much as I did. She seemed to like when I would comb her hair, brush her teeth and help her get dressed. The staff was often annoyed by me because I was anal in making sure her clothes were properly labeled with her name. I spent a lot of time in the laundry room looking for clothes that didn't make it back to her drawers and closet. I got the biggest joy from decorating her room. I tried to make sure she had plenty of family pictures, flowers and any personal items to make it her home. Wilma and I both insisted on having a radio in her room because we knew she loved music. The most memorable times were the visits during holidays. The facility always did an outstanding job celebrating holidays and resident birthdays. This was especially appreciated when they suggested we cease taking her home or removing her from the facility.

When she was at home with us it was like she was still living with us. Although I was pleased with her progress, she still had some incidents at the unit, but they were manageable. I felt secure and confident that she was getting her meds and adjusting well. She was going to the movies and had regularly scheduled hair and nail appointments. I felt like she was living the quality of life she deserved. She was enjoying life and I thought she felt that way as well.

She would occasionally mention she was not going to continue to live there, but that was only the disease talking. I would hear her say every now and then that she was going home with me. There were times when I had to distract her to leave the floor, but she'd always be comfortable there when I left, which was reassuring. A few times when I would visit her, she would be talking with the nurses at the nurse's station. She even thought she was one of the nurses. They would play along with her. I thought it was cute. They would share with me about Ms. Helen's dancing. They all thought she was a great dancer and wanted to know her story, especially when a new nurse would come to the unit because my mom was still very young. We had decorated her room and there were plenty of pictures of her in her younger years. She was absolutely beautiful. The crew at my mom's facility would always take an interest in the patient's past. Marilyn did a great job making her room feel like a home. We made a poster board of all the important people in her life, including her mother, sisters, brothers, son, daughters, grandkids, and cousins. I would point out a person on the board and ask if she knew them. This helped me keep track of the progression of her memory loss. We took her home a lot, even when there was a warning to evacuate for a hurricane threat. We wouldn't let them take her, although it meant additional work for the staff. I wanted her with me. They had to get her meds in order, make sure she had enough, and that I understood how to administer them. We felt like she was healthy enough physically, but I still had a fear of her being away from me outside of the walls of this building.

Eventually, the staff expressed their concern that taking her home so often was confusing her. She needed stability, especially as she progressed into new stages. They informed me it was becoming too stressful for her. Her recovery time was taking longer upon her return to the facility. I struggled with their request because I was still hung up on the fact that she was in a nursing home. Guilt started to consume me. Marilyn noticed that I was getting depressed and consuming myself with questions that only one person could answer.

On my 42nd birthday, she brought me a beautiful Life Application Study Bible that came in a black suede carrying case. When she handed it to me, she made it clear that I needed to rely on my faith more, pray and let go. Marilyn was constantly reassuring me that I was a good daughter and the situation with my mother was different from other people's journey with an elderly mom. I was convinced that I had equipped myself with the armor needed to soldier up in this battle that God had placed before me. It was truly a battle because as my mom's dementia progressed, there were several emergency room visits. Some of the trips were very scary, but none like the first time she went.

They called to say she was lethargic and did not want to get out of bed. Her pressure was low and they asked if someone could meet them there. If not, they would have a staff member stay with her. I was coaching one of Bailey's basketball games at the time and had to leave. Marilyn was at the game also as a team mom. I rushed to the hospital, which was about an hour away. It didn't matter that they'd said it would be a while before they got there. We were in the city at a tournament, coaching was the one thing that brought me a sense of peace and calmness. I loved coaching basketball and enjoyed teaching people about the game that I loved. It was my sanctuary. I would often think about the coaches I had throughout high school and how much they meant to me and taught me many life lessons. To me it was about self-esteem and them knowing their value either as a ball player or a person in society. For every hour I coached, it was an hour I didn't have to be that over consumed, over worked, and the daughter of a sick mom.

There was always a process to take a resident from the facility to the hospital. By the time I got there she had just arrived and I was able to go in with her. She was dazed, inattentive, her eyes were unfocused, and she didn't acknowledge I was there. I was scared as I'd never seen her like that. They took her to the back and started with an I.V. I wanted to go to the back, but they asked me to wait. I told them she needed me because she was not going to be able to communicate effectively. I kept asking was she hurting.

When I finally got to the back, she didn't recognize me at all. I grabbed her hand and started rubbing the back of it. Repeatedly, I asked her if she was okay, but she didn't respond. I just kept rubbing her hand and reassuring her of my presence. Finally, she started to come around a little bit. She looked at me and asked if I knew her. I said "Yes, old lady; you are my mama, Ms. Helen." I would always speak with my mother in a joking manner because I wanted her to always feel at ease. Then she smiled and said, "Oh yeah, I know you."

The doctor said my mom had a urinary tract infection and those infections were extremely tough for dementia patients. Then he shared, "We treat this a lot with patients from nursing homes, but it's rougher for patients with dementia. We will get her back on track and back to the facility tonight." I needed to go outside for a minute just to get myself together. I went to my truck and was sitting there in a full-blown crying fit to the point I was repeatedly asking myself why. Why is she going through this? I was questioning God.

Then my cell phone rang and it was one of my player's mom on the other end of the call. I tried to make it a point to answer whenever one of my players or their parents needed to talk to me. I had to stop crying, but I guess she could tell in my voice that I was having a moment. She wanted to check on me and find out how my mom was doing. I told her everything was fine and thanked her for calling. Before I could hang up, she asked if she could pray with me. As she began to pray, I started to cry and scream. I screamed so much she started yelling through the phone, "Coach! Coach! Are you by yourself? Let me come to you." I could tell she was worried; I assured her I was fine and once again thanked her for calling. Now it was time to return inside to my mom.

My mother's health was declining and things were starting to change. She recognized my face, but not my name. Our visits now involved me playing music for her, clipping her toenails, and telling her about the business. She wasn't really engaged. I would talk with her as if she understood everything I was saying. There were also times when she didn't know who Marilyn was. It didn't matter to me that my mom didn't know who I was. I knew who I was and most importantly I knew who she was.

Marilyn and I attended Christmas dinner at the facility in December of 2010, as we had done all the previous years. My mom had lost weight and wasn't talking much. She was now being pushed around in a wheelchair. Her face had started to sink in from the weight loss. I would kiss her on the forehead as if she had asked me a hundred times to do it. The doctor was there that night making his rounds. The nurse informed that he needed to talk to me. He explained how these new symptoms were indicative of the Stage 7 phase, and that her lack of eating would only get worse.

After that she would be at the end of her life cycle. I needed to know how long that would be, but he couldn't tell me exactly. He did state that we needed to select the company that would provide hospice care for her. He also needed to know if I wanted to have her fed intravenously when she completely stopped eating. Of course, I did. He further explained how that would prolong her pain as she passed through. We wouldn't know the amount of pain she would be in because she couldn't tell us, but it could be managed if we liked. "Your mom deserves to die with dignity. Sometimes loved ones hold on for themselves when it may not be what's best for the patient." He told me he would do whatever my friend and I decided was best. This facility was one of the places that was fully aware that Marilyn and I were together. They knew the truth. While we had lied to so many, we needed this place to know that Marilyn was just as important as I was when it came to the care of my mother. There were no gray areas between us on this.

Chapter 29 ~ A Break in the Rainbow

After asking her did she love her, the details she shared made it obvious that this woman was trying to destroy what we had worked so hard to build. I had to consider the affair along with us starting a business.

* * *

My mother's illness may have been my motivation to start a business to change my family's fortune. I needed to prepare myself for the abundance of blessings I expected. Part of that preparation included reading, studying, and analyzing. A few books I read to prepare myself for the things I was expecting and claiming included:

1. *Richest Man in Babylon* by George Clason
2. *The Millionaire Next Door* by Thomas J Stanley, William D Danko
3. *Think and Grow Rich: The Original* by Napoleon Hill
4. *The Rage of a Privileged Class* by Ellis Cose

Ever since I was a child, I was determined not to be a victim of my circumstances. I would dream and pretend to escape the shame and guilt I was carrying. I would prepare myself for every encounter. Starting this business was no different except I had pushed myself harder to launch this business, because I wanted my mom to witness it. I was 100% confident that we would be a success. The one thought that excited me the most was the possibility that my mom could reap some of the benefits to add to the quality of her life.

My military life had equipped me to be a leader. Coaching had taught me how to blend different talents together to achieve a goal. Being a letter carrier helped me understand the importance of customer service and making a connection with the people I served. I thought back to Mr. Walter and how he used his business to uplift, help, and give opportunities to people who may not have been given one. Living in the south, having a black-owned construction company in the 80's and hiring black kids and women, made him truly a change agent.

Marilyn was concerned about starting a business because of the potential cost. I understood what that meant. We had to choose a business venture with a very low start-up cost. I looked at a possible franchise, but I quickly realized that wouldn't work. We needed to work at our own pace and keep our circle close. I had to approach this thing like I had approached everything else that was dear to me. This business would be another link in the chain of successful endeavors that made us wealthy. I knew what wealth felt like because of Marilyn and the girls. There was an abundance of love in my life, but I needed to add some money to that wealth. I understood that it was important to build a group of people to be the foundation of our business. We needed to be well-rounded so we could reach the full potential of growth for this new baby in our lives.

We opened the doors of our business on August 11, 2006. Yes, this was a little more than a year before my mother entered the facility. Our first year was slow, and we were a negative $26 in sales. We didn't do much of anything. The next year we had our first official job cleaning carpet for one of my co-workers at the post office who wanted to help me out. Everyone in the office was curious as to how the business was doing. I don't think many thought it was going anywhere because I was still working a lot of hours. I spent most of my first few months registering us with city, state, and federal government agencies. Our first couple of jobs were all residential with friends we knew.

Then we got a call from a federal agency looking for a small business to clean a few military recruiting offices. We thought we had hit the jack pot until we started submitting bids. We realized we needed a whole lot of recruiting stations to cash in on anything. Thankfully, the connections gained from my postal route proved to be very beneficial. My previous customers appreciated the time I took to talk and spend time with them. Remember the elderly lady on my route, Ms. Hernandez? She was the woman that would have me read her important mail because she didn't trust her sons to get the right information to her. I asked her if she would mind helping me with my new cleaning business. She was ecstatic to be a part of a new family business.

Then later in the year, Alexis had a friend who was over business development for a major cleaning company located in Houston. They were looking for subcontractors to clean retail stores for a major cell phone company. We hadn't been in business that long and didn't know if we could handle it, but couldn't turn down the opportunity when we hadn't really had any business. We needed to purchase more equipment. I went to a couple of pawn shops on my route and purchased buffers and commercial carpet cleaning machines.

We started subcontracting for them in October of 2007 with a few stores, which was our second year in business. Things were starting to pick up because of the work Ms. Hernandez was doing at those four military recruiting stations. The government offered us twelve more offices. Our subcontracting work with the other company was picking up as well. We needed to hire more people. The family cleaned at night at some of the stores, but we were getting too many and needed more help. Our business was growing tremendously. I started to get anxious about the growth of the business. I felt hindered because I was still working full-time at the post office, spending time with my mom remained a priority, as well as coaching basketball.

Ms. Hernandez had been a blessing to my business like so many of my customers on the route. The word got around on my route that I had a business, and it was doing well. Many of my customers were happy and wanted to be a part of the growth. But there were a few that saw my business as an opportunity for them. A mother of a young man on my route started to take notice of me.

At first, I thought she was being nice because I would spend time talking with her son about school and sports. He told her about me and how he thought I was cool. The attention his mother was giving me was much more than just being nice . She was flirting with me every day and leaving messages in her mailbox for me. What started out as curiosity would turn into a manipulative emotional roller coaster that would test the strength and resolve of my relationship with Marilyn. I had allowed myself to be taken advantage of financially and emotionally. Marilyn had always been the protector of my soul. But how was I to tell her something that would break her heart. She was my best friend and I had to tell her.

I had fallen down and I couldn't find a way to get back up. After I told her, the only question Marilyn asked me was, "Do you love her?" Of course, I didn't love her and I told Marilyn that.

~MJ's Journey~

*After asking her did she love her, the details she shared made it obvious that this woman was trying to destroy what we had worked so hard to build. I had to consider the affair along with us starting a business. As things evolved, our relationship was jeopardized by arguments, the deceit, and the lies. This girl and her family tried to wreck what we had. Eventually, the mistress began to turn this into a game. I made it clear to Wilma that I was open to listen to her and to try and understand what happened. I asked questions to help me understand if what we had was salvageable. I didn't condone what Wilma had done, but I definitely was not going to allow anybody to sabotage our relationship or mistreat her. This was absolutely the most difficult time in my life. No illness, death or misfortune compared to the pain this brought. I eventually accepted this as **karma**. That was the only way I could make sense of my pain and broken heart.*

Even with the heartache caused, she was not going to let anyone take advantage of me. Marilyn was the smartest person I knew, and she had an impeccable intellectual ability to maneuver us out of dangerous situations. I knew she loved me and could feel the desperation because I had put everything at risk. I had put her in a position she had never been in before and it caused her to question my love for her. I was the person that never lied to her, the person she trusted the most. She put all those emotions to the side to once again, help me find my way out of a sunken place like she had done some twenty years ago. After telling Marilyn about my foolish mistake, we would never be the same but I prayed we would always be together.

In 2010, I was working full-time for the business. My official last day at the post office was January 15, 2010 on Martin Luther King Day. It was also eleven months prior to the doctor at the Christmas party telling me that my mom was now entering Stage 7 of dementia. I'd left a secure government job to run our family business full-time and we were really nervous. Marilyn and I had previously decided that we were going to wait for the business to reach a particular point in monthly sales before I left the post office. We agreed it was time after four years into the business. I had been at the post office for 11 years and given 10 years to the military, which meant I had a total of 21 years of federal service. I had the years of service, but not the age. I was 46 years old, but too young to retire. My only option was to resign. We worried about how this would affect receiving my postal service retirement. After doing much research, I found that I could resign and delay my retirement benefits until I reached my required age.

Leaving the post office meant no more medical insurance, which resulted in me paying for COBRA insurance at a crazy amount. When my COBRA ended, it was the first time I'd ever been without insurance in over 20 years. Since I was a disabled veteran, I qualified to receive services through the Department of Veteran Affairs. Of course, Marilyn had insurance, but she could not add me to her benefits. Having been together for over twenty years, we were prime examples of domestic partners. Yet we were still separate in the eyes of the system. A couple of years later, Marilyn's company was one of the few to offer domestic partner insurance, at which time she was able to add me.

The business was doing well. We were receiving many accolades and awards. We were featured in a Houston monthly magazine about Veteran Owned businesses. We were also selected as one of the few companies in Houston to participate in the initial class for the Goldman Sachs 10,000 Small Initiative Program. This was the beginning of our business receiving much needed exposure.

The business may have been doing well but my mother was dying. Marilyn and I were battling for our relationship. It was going through a storm and teetering on the brink of dissolving. We knew we loved each other, but how were we going to continue to be in love. During one of Marilyn's mother's scheduled stays, with Marilyn's sibling in Atlanta, she suffered a stroke. She flew to Atlanta to assist with the recovery. Her mother's health was declining. She had gone through many medical emergencies throughout her life.

The day before Marilyn left to visit her mother, we selected the hospice company that would care for my mom. Her body was beginning to shut down and we were down to the last few days. I had promised myself and her that I would not let her die alone. By this time, Marilyn and I were very fragile and worn down. The emotional and physical breakdown that came from caring for sick parents, to a broken relationship we were trying to fix, began to take a toll on both of us.

While she was in hospice, I sat by her bedside and continued to work the business. My mother wasn't particularly a religious person, but she believed in God. I don't want to sound presumptuous and assume anything about her relationship with Him, but I did find comfort in the thought that my mom was going to heaven. I would leave every night at 10:00 p.m. A few times the nurses would let me stay a little later, but I would return first thing the next morning. Since my mom had a nurse dedicated to her, I didn't have to be there around the clock, but I wanted to spend as much time by her side.

It was just after 1:00 a.m. on Sunday Aug 21, 2011, when my cell phone rang. The nurse said I should probably come right away because they were not sure how much longer it would be. Marilyn was scheduled to return to Houston that day around 3:00 pm. The doctor and staff had done an excellent job estimating my mom's passing. I jumped out of the bed and started the longest 30-minute drive of my life. I called Marilyn and she talked me through the dreadful ride while trying to switch to an earlier flight back to Houston. When I arrived at the facility and exited the elevator all the wonderful nurses and faces that I had grown to love met me at the doorway, staring with a look of deep sadness. I thought I had gotten there too late. I rushed into my mom's room and the hospice nurse was there with her. My mom was still passing through the final stage of life. I grabbed her hands because I wanted her to know I was there – I am here mama.

I had never called her mama. All my life I called her by her first name. But this day I needed her to know I'd kept my promise. I had to call family members for them to say goodbye to her. I called my sister and then my Aunt Jean. Aunt Heavenly had passed a few years earlier. That was something I never told my mother while she was battling this disease. I didn't know what that might have done to her. I also called Uncle Steve, her big cousin/brother. Marilyn also made phone calls. She called Alexis and asked her to head to Texas City to comfort "Auntie". Shortly after I arrived, there was a gentle knock at the door and there she was, my sweet Alexis. Bailey was in school, which was an hour and a half away, but she headed home as soon as she heard.

My mother started to gasp for air and her breathing became much more difficult. I stood next to her and began to read Psalm 23 over and over. I kept telling her how sorry I was that this disease had done this to her. Finally, at 10:48 a.m., on Sunday, Aug 21, 2011, my mama, my shero, took her last breath. As I wept and sobbed like the motherless child that I now was, my baby girl held me up. As she witnessed the person that she always knew to be tough as nails, completely fall apart. Alexis stayed by my side and comforted me.

Suddenly, the tears stopped. The only words that repeatedly came from my mouth were, 'Okay, okay, okay,' because my mom was now free and going home. It was time to celebrate her life and give her a homegoing with the dignity she deserved. It was my time to honor her, as the daughter she trusted. I was grateful that I had been able to spend those last years with her. The facility knew who to call because those arrangements had been made when I agreed to hospice care.

Also, years of coaching had put some very special people in my life. One of the families that was very dear to me, owned a funeral business. I requested them to take care of my mother and send her to Arkansas, where she would be put to rest. The nurses kept telling me it was time to leave because there was nothing else I could do. They needed to begin preparing my mom's body to be picked up. I left the room, but refused to leave the floor until they brought my mother from her room. I felt as though I was still responsible for her until she got home.

As I left the floor, many of the nurses consoled me. They had done right by my mom and had my back the entire time she was there. I went home and laid in the bed, not crying, just thinking. It was strange because I was lying there and wondering... wondering what my mom was doing.

Marilyn rushed through the door, headed upstairs and held me in her arms. We both cried and cried. She felt bad that she wasn't there with me. I was just relieved that she still wanted to even be there for me.

It was at that moment we both realized that we had lived this life together, but apart. We had never been present in this love affair and we needed to fix that. We had given each other the prime years of our lives, but had lived much of it in the shadows. We had not truly basked in the authenticity of our love story. We agreed we both wanted to change that, but for now we had another priority, preparing my mom's homegoing and celebrating her life.

Marilyn and I were in much better shape financially and fully prepared to handle my mother's funeral cost. I had a paid life insurance policy that my grandmother made me promise to take out and keep up. Thankfully, it was the one thing I paid consistently. I had taken out a $10,000 policy that my grandmother was adamant about maintaining. When we talked throughout the years before her death, she would ask about it regularly.

My mother had a beautiful homegoing fit for the queen she was. The entire Houston family loaded up to take the 10-hour drive to Arkansas to celebrate her life. Marilyn continued to stand by my side. She shielded me, she held me, and she prayed with me and for me.

Chapter 30 ~ Rainbow Complete

We were prepared to not survive as a couple... As the girls grew older, things began to change. Now we were here – two broken, battle-beaten souls trying to hold on to the only thing we knew – each other.

** * *

~MJ's Journey~

Caring for our ailing and aging moms was not an easy task. It was also one we were not prepared for. We were not prepared because our relationship was in shambles. Finances were better, but not great. Not to mention that Wilma's mom was supposed to have many more earthly years. It tugged at my heart that I wasn't by her side when Helen passed. That was to be something that we were to go through together, no matter what. It was an unspoken rule. The celebration of Helen's transition was classy, unflawed and all that she deserved. The ride to Arkansas was bittersweet. We were all thankful that our schedules managed to gel so we could be there for Wilma and each other.

One of the many wonderful things about living in Houston, TX is its diversity. During our time living here, we have experienced many night clubs, restaurants and much of the entertainment it has to offer. It has an entire district within the city that celebrates the LGBTQ community. When our friends visited us from New Orleans and Arkansas, we took pride in taking them to areas where they were comfortable and could completely enjoy themselves. With Houston being one of the most liberal cities in the country, it allowed us to find a therapist that counseled same-sex couples. It was important for us to have a counselor that understood that our relationship was just like any other. We went into an intense therapy program. We paid out-of-pocket for the first two months until Marilyn's job began to offer insurance coverage for domestic partners. We had to commit to the program and there was no room to miss appointments. We knew we had to do this. I was now working full-time with the business and any time I took away from the business was time not generating income. Marilyn was still working, but she was the primary financer of the business. She would fund the payroll and buy the supplies when we would fall short. Any time we spent not working was a direct hit to our pockets.

Neither one of us wanted to walk away from the relationship we had worked so hard to make sense of. We had spent our entire adult life together. During this time, we raised two girls, bought a house, and had started a business. We also buried my mom and was still caring for her mom. This was bigger than us, but I was not naïve to think that she wasn't questioning who I was.

~MJ's Journey~

Going to counseling was not something I had ever heard of. At this point, I was desperate. I never stopped praying, but in the midst of prayer, I desperately yearned for additional survival tools. I needed help in making sure I was doing all that I could to protect my girls. I wanted the therapist to provide a miracle solution. A fix for the lies I was living, the mixed emotions I was battling and most importantly, the piercing pain in my heart that I could not bear.

I had never gone to a therapist or any type of counseling. While I expected to talk about Marilyn, I was not expecting to share much about me and my childhood. I was only prepared to talk about everything related to saving my relationship with Marilyn with hopes of receiving resources to fix it... at any cost. I expected to do what it took to make things right. I hadn't completely talked about my childhood to anyone. I never shared how certain emotions, my sense of uneasiness and fears were all related to my childhood. I had only unloaded most of those details with Marilyn, but had not even given her all of it. I never wanted to peel those raw emotions back because I was afraid that sharing my insecurities would inflict more hurt and pain. I was not willing to unfold those feelings, because of the challenging but much needed self-made adjustments done along this journey. I had fixed, in me, what I could, licked my wounds and kept on going.

I wasn't going to get off that easy in these counseling sessions. A lot of what was happening in our relationship were things that happened because of my inability to come to grips with what I needed. A large part of my issues was from my childhood trauma. Often times people go through trauma and still manage to function as a productive citizen, and I was one of them, at least in the eyes of society. I needed to be more than that. I desired to be a complete person... to be visible and heard.

I spoke my truth about the things that happened to me and the things I had done to people. The same question kept surfacing, "How does all of this make you feel?" I really couldn't address that because I never really expressed or truly identified how things made me feel. Eventually, the therapist asked the ultimate question, "Had I forgiven myself?" I didn't know how to respond to that either, but I knew what she meant. I was smart enough to know that what happened to me as a child wasn't my fault, but understood exactly what she meant.

It was my personal duty to protect myself and to do that; I absolutely had to forgive myself. I had never addressed how I felt about any of the abuse or mistreatments because I thought I was to go-along-to-get-along. Whether any of my failures were large or small, when things didn't go according to plan, failure to me was magnified. I had taken this approach with the intent of protecting my feelings and minimizing any disappointments. When and if I failed, it was me that had let myself down. I made up in my mind that no person would ever have control over my well-being. I would also protect any and everybody that was important to me. It wasn't just about being there for others, it was about protecting me and those that made me a priority.

There was no place in my heart to let others see the emotional things that hurt me because I had one job in my life and that was to survive and protect. That is why I waited up at nights for my mom to come home. That is why I feared leaving for college because my little sister would have to fend for herself. I had years of emotional baggage built up in my heart, and feared I was on the brink of losing everything. The therapist asked me if I had told my mom about the things that happened to me. When I asked which one, she looked at me with astonishment. In that moment she knew I had a lot of bones buried yet to be uncovered.

I did tell my mom later when I was grown and before she got sick, at the encouragement of my Aunt Heavenly. My mother wanted to know why I didn't tell her as a child and all I could say was that I needed my mother. I knew if I had told her, she would have gone to jail and then I wouldn't have her. I needed her because she loved me more than anyone had ever loved me. My mother was extremely shaken when I told her the news. She kept saying, "I wish you had told me." My mother, in a rare moment of tenderness, asked me, "Don't you know that I would have never let anyone hurt you?" I told her I knew that. She apologized to me and told me she hated that I had carried so much around for so many years. I knew she would never let anybody intentionally hurt me. Yet, I felt like I had let someone hurt me, that was my thought process. I would never let anybody intentionally hurt me again and that's how I lived my life. I had carried this around, but then an angel was sent to watch over me. That angel was Marilyn.

But now I had placed a heavy burden on her to be my chief consoler, not recognizing she was going through her own personal reckoning. She was a woman that had been known all her life as a straight, beautiful, black woman. She had married a man that many saw as her love that was meant to be. They had been together since teenagers. She had children with him, but she had left her husband to be with a woman. She was raised up in church by a religious family, believed in the Trinity, and believed in the words of the Bible as interpreted by many.

There we were, two young girls, placing our lives in each

other's hands. Neither one of us were equipped to fix the other, but believed it was our destiny. I had given her the stability, protection, and kindness she deserved. She had given me the care, love and loyalty I needed. But we both needed to address the things that kept us from being a total and complete person. We had relied on each other for everything, and now we were broken. Marilyn couldn't fix my shame and insecurity. I couldn't fix her guilt. We had protected each other's hearts, but we hadn't explored or lived the endless love we had for each other. Hiding, lying, and living a "normal life" had us living the most abnormal life. We never questioned the path we took, we just hoped and prayed it was the right one.

We were prepared to not survive as a couple, but we were not prepared for our girls to not survive the life we had chosen. We fought every day for them to be accepted without judgement, which was our motivation to survive. As the girls grew older, things began to change. Now we were here – two broken, battle-beaten souls trying to hold on to the only thing we knew – each other.

~MJ's Journey~

During therapy, I discovered that we both had layers and layers of hurt, baggage and shame. Some which had been created in our relationship that was covering up childhood and young adult pain. It was in the sessions that these layers were peeled back one by one. The therapist was great at penetrating to the core as she met with us individually and collectively. When we counseled together, I learned that I had, unknowingly, shut Wilma out while I dealt with my personal confusion. I was struggling with whether I would be discarded by God and had I forsaken Him? If I allowed what man thought and believed, I would have been doomed from day one. I am thankful and so grateful that I have a personal relationship with God that no man can separate.

We both thought we understood each other's paths. Hell, we had walked it together for many years – at least we thought we had. What I thought was my strength had quickly become my weakness. What I had seen as a strength in Marilyn had become her weakness. We had made this PACT to live this life and yet, we had cut off the oxygen we needed to grow as individuals. I had convinced myself that I had given Marilyn everything I had promised. She had convinced herself she only needed so much to survive. During an intense session with our therapist, it was determined we were both wrong. The therapist asked how it made me feel again. This time it was about the PACT. How did it make me feel? Did I feel invisible again? I never thought I had felt invisible with Marilyn.

She made it clear to me that is what I had been doing all these years – being invisible because I was not addressing my emotions. She asked Marilyn how it felt to have such a wonderful companion in her life and not be able to tell the world because of fear. We both had been living in fear and the one thing that gave us the most joy and comfort, was now the leading cause of that fear. My love was now being questioned. Was our love strong enough to survive this? Maybe what led me down the road that got us here was the fear of everything changing.

We no longer needed the PACT. The girls were bigger, and Marilyn would no longer need me. Was I preparing myself to be okay again, as I had done before when the pain of something was too much to face? I had heard many times, from others, throughout our journey that she would eventually go back to being straight and maybe even to her husband. The therapist asked Marilyn how it made her feel to hear that.

~MJ's Journey~

*I told the therapist that I was sick of Wilma constantly worrying about me going back to my husband. I jumped up from the chair and screamed, "What you should understand is, I don't need you; I want you! Since the day we were 19 years old, sitting on your aunt's sofa, you have been the single most conflict in my life. I have questioned everything about me because of you. If I wanted to not love you, I couldn't because I did not want to lose you." How could someone constantly have the fear that their love would be lost to the person they took them from. I guess it's also called the fear of **karma**.*

The therapist then said, "You two have to cut each other some slack. You are a living, loving entity, and you two have a romance that's waiting to breathe. Start living your romance. You are just two girls who love each other. That's called life. Let go and live your destiny. Society and your family's beliefs have convinced you both that you are not worthy of this love, but you are. We both looked at each other with tears in our eyes. We had gone through hell together with this ordeal. Then I saw that beautiful 13-year-old girl that I had been crushing on since day one. She was my girl, and I almost lost her to my stupidity and our inability to love each other without fear.

~MJ's Journey~

Although our relationship was at a crossroads, I was determined to salvage our family unit. During the therapy sessions, we were both raw in our expressions on the why's and what for's. I was still battling the decision of "coming out" and Wilma also struggled with living in secret. She needed outward confirmation, something to identify with so that others would know the family that she celebrated daily... her family.

Wilma was constantly concerned with me going back to my husband. That bothered me and it bothered me really bad. Her constant comments and questions were annoying. They were intolerable because it made it difficult for me to convince her that me going back to him should never be her worry. Her concern should have been where mine was. I needed help navigating this new life and not feeling as though I had to prove something to somebody. I made myself believe that I had to be like others in order to be accepted in the circle of people that I wanted to be in, and wanted my girls to be a part of. In order to be like others, I convinced myself that I had to lie. My lies went beyond hiding in the closet. They were completely made up, fabricated lives. The things I did and said to create another life was exhausting. I created and made up relationships with the opposite sex. Lies that I would tell gentlemen callers to prevent them from thinking something was "wrong" with me. It had all been too much.

Marilyn came into my life for a reason and we have loved each other through many seasons – seasons of struggle, loss, failure, redemption, and forgiveness. Now it was time to embrace who and what we were.

Since 1985 we had lived in the shadows and behind a wall of shame. There was no need to make a grand "coming out" announcement. We would now just live in our truth. We released an energy within us that had been buried way too long. We are just a story of two people who fell in love, but we had been conditioned to hate the label that had been given to our type of love. We buried the people behind the label because of shame, never allowing our true persons to surface.

We are all just a story being told, but when we label and demonize the person behind the stories, we lessen their existence. Marilyn and I no longer would accept such demonization that society tried to place on us and if that meant we would lose someone along the way, we were fine with that. We owed only two people an explanation for the decisions we made and why we made them.

~MJ's Journey~

The day we told the girls our truth was still a day that was not complete. They received it just as I had expected. They made it clear that they loved us unconditionally and nothing could change that, especially the choices made to protect them and our unit. I tried to explain why I made the decisions that I did, but I did not want it to appear that it was because of my failed relationship with their dad. I owed it to them to know that I chose to not try and fix what their dad and I had. Whether it was because I found it unfixable or if it was simply because I didn't want to try. It didn't matter because their dad and I had made it quite obvious that we were not interested in each other or the relationship. We had both gone our separate ways much earlier than the physical parting. We can all spend time blaming each other, when the bottom line is… it just didn't work.

We had freed ourselves and we started to live in the moment of our love story, and oh boy what a story it was? Our house had become a home. Our family was finally allowed to be accepting or rejecting of us. What we had not realized, was they had already accepted us. They were just waiting on us to do the same. We had slowly normalized our family.

Our business went to another level. We grew from three employees to 50 employees and 10 vendors within a year. We expanded the services we provided. Soon after graduating, Bailey began working full-time for the company and Alexis managed the books while working her full-time job. Marilyn finally unleashed her natural given talents and was doing many of the things she loved. She also became a member of the American Marriage Ministries with a focus on officiating same-sex marriages. She actually officiated our goddaughter's wedding.

We were no longer running and hiding and began to reconnect with things that once brought us pain. We tried to capture every moment of our love in pictures just like my uncle had requested. We joined organizations that we'd stayed away from in the past. We felt that we were being blessed and were determined to give back as much as we could. We wanted to be a blessing in other people's lives. Alexis and her hubby had our first grandchild in July 2014. Our second grandchild arrived in 2020. Our lives had come full circle. We were who we were. Marilyn was a beautiful, black woman in love with another beautiful, black woman and we were a hellified force together because we chose each other. We raised two strong, black women, started a successful business together, and were as connected as connected could be.

In August of 2014, Marilyn made it known that she wanted to make sure that I never felt invisible again and wanted to marry the love of her life.

~MJ's Journey~

After all the hurt, broken promises, arguments, affair, and therapy sessions, I knew that true healing would only happen if we made a real commitment to each other. I wanted to define our relationship and seal our love by the ocean. The ocean symbolizes chaos with no definite form. It also represents the beginning of life and stability. Since we are both lovers of water and its representation of life and freedom, I asked Wilma to marry me and to plan for us to do it on the beach in California, where we would leave the chaos and embrace our freedom – even it was still just for us.

On September 5th, 2014, we exchanged vows at the foot of Ocean Avenue in the sand facing the Pacific Ocean in Carmel Beach, California. We wrote our vows and recited them to each other in the presence of two witnesses. We didn't have fancy wedding rings. We purchased elastic wedding bands from the Walmart in Salinas, California. Yes, we were married nine months before marriage equality was passed nationwide. It didn't matter to us. We wanted to live this love affair out loud. It just felt right. We drove from the coast of Northern California to Southern California that day after we promised to love and honor each other forever. I was riding the coast of California with the woman that had captured my heart since I was a kid.

Now we were 50 years old, starting our lives together as a married couple. All the lies were behind us, all the stereotypical chains that had bound us were no longer holding us back. As I looked in her face, I realized that everything I had hoped and dreamt for as a child had come true and I had a family to love and one that loved me. We were each other's princess' in shining armor.

We enjoy watching the young people today that are free and open to who they are. We also know that in some communities it's still hard to truly accept that. When we think about the time and era in which we were discovering who we were, we don't know if we would have done anything different because each journey is personal. Just because it's personal doesn't mean you shouldn't be seen. My walk was for me and only me – that little black girl born in the south who grew up in the projects of Chicago.

I thought everything about me was wrong. Who would believe it? That I would find another little black girl in Arkansas – a little black girl that was just like me, looking for a kinder heart to love in her image as well.

And for that I say to all... Love is blind, Love is kind, Love is not perfect, but if you love with all your heart, love has no limits on time... "LOVE ALWAYS WINS"!

Rainbow Complete!

Our Two Cents

We hid the experiences of this true love story, while hiding all the best there was about both of us. We shut off the part of the world that cared, but did this to protect our children, our lives and our journey.

As life continued to happen, we realized we dismissed those that would have enjoyed taking this ride with us. Some would have celebrated us, but also those that didn't respect our path. We knew that those people were in a special category with all the deep south Bible belt teachings, especially in our community. With everything else, things evolved and at the end of the day, we know now that we lived a "traditional love story". We have typical relationship conflicts, we cared for and buried our parents, built a business and reared two girls that became two awesome adults. We experienced a love that for years we could only share with each other – just the four of us.

POEM FOR MY MOM

It's been a hard fight, but a fight worth fighting. It's not up to us to question why. We live the life we are given, and we play the hand we've been dealt. You put up a good fight and now you're home. Time is an expansion of movement over a period of events. Your time here was precious and much too short, but you lived your life to the fullest. A person is measured by the people they have touched in this journey called life. Your journey touched many and will continue to be touched by others. You gave ME breath and God blessed me with the honor of watching you take YOUR last breath. It was my love for my friend and the unbreakable bond for my mother that kept me praying and hoping that you would be free of this struggle that had taken over your body and mind. Aug 21, 2011 was a day of rejoice for me; for my mother was going home and free from the struggles of this earthly life. I will miss your flesh, but your spirit will forever be with me. So, for now, I wish you farewell or better yet, a simple I'll see you later. Until we meet again, I will cherish our memories and continue to take pride in being your daughter and I will do my best to honor your legacy.

God Bless... See you on the other side.... Wilma Jean

About the Authors

Naomi W. Scales and Marilyn J. Jordan, authors of **From Pain to Love: Our Journey Outside the Rainbow,** hope that sharing their story will bring encouragement to others, the will to embrace authenticity, to live out loud, and an understanding that rainbows follow the darkest storms.

Naomi, affectionately known as Wilma, and Marilyn are the owners of MarFran Cleaning, LLC located in Houston, Texas. In existence since 2006, their business offers janitorial services, lawncare and general contracting, both locally and nationally. They have expanded their business to include two additional companies, MarFran-Apex and MarFran Communication.

They have often shared their experiences with likewise individuals. Marilyn is duly ordained through *American Marriage Ministry* with emphasis on same-sex marriages. Both ladies have appeared as invited guests on *The Oprah Winfrey Show*, sharing their experiences and expertise with the viewers and studio audiences.

www.ingramcontent.com/pod-product-compliance
Lightning Source LLC
Chambersburg PA
CBHW051707160426
43209CB00004B/1057